Bethany is one amazing instructor and students flock to her classes at Shoreline Community College's Continuing Education Department! Bethany's student evaluations are always excellent and the book that she wrote is extremely valuable. Plus, she always has a smile. During these economic times, Bethany's class is worth every penny and helps community members supplement their income.

—Cynthia Johnson, Director (**www.shoreline.edu/ce**)

Bethany helps make the daunting task of creating a Web "identity" a breeze! She is generous with her time and talents and has gently pulled me kicking and screaming into this new online world. I never would have/could have launched my website without her. She makes me feel that anything is possible! My experience with her has been nothing short of amazing. I'm glad that she is now part of my "team," and I look forward to doing the next step in my promotional homework with her. I feel I have only just scratched the surface of her knowledge, and I can't wait to see what is next!

—Sandy Anderson (**www.dreamingdanecatering.com**)

Bethany is extremely knowledgeable about mystery shopping and similar employment opportunities. Her presentation was enthusiastic and realistic. I especially appreciated the book she provided with listings of real companies to get started with. She obviously enjoys sharing her experience and knowledge, and anyone would benefit from her classes.

—Anonymous student review through Canton Adult Education

When my website needed a makeover, I called on Bethany to do the job. As soon as we began to outline the scope of the project, I found that her knowledge of Web best practices, honed from personal experience and research, is amazing. She not only followed my directions but took the initiative to add features that enhanced the marketing value. She's energetic, creative, personable, a hard-working entrepreneur, and a top-notch professional.

—Lori Stephens, pNLP, CCP (**www.verbatimeditorial.com**)

I really enjoyed Bethany's presentation! The information was comprehensive, well organized and thought out. Bethany was easy to follow and constantly asked if we had questions, making sure we all understood each concept before moving onto the next subject. She was amazingly knowledgeable and gave us numerous resources to pursue after class. I am highly impressed with her professionalism and was amazed that an adult education class could be so outstanding. She belongs on the lecture circuit!

—Anonymous student review through Dearborn Adult Education

For the past five years, Bethany has helped my practice with all things marketing. She has polished up our website, outlined a marketing calendar, created marketing products, and has given us a much stronger Web presence. She is professional, efficient, highly effective, has an understated depth of knowledge, and explains the information so anyone can understand and use the information. If you need help with any type of small business development and want to have a good time doing it, Bethany can make it happen.

—Dr. Bonnie Verhunce (**www.VitalityChiropractic.com**)

Bethany exceeded my expectations and gave me all the information I wanted and more. I took both her mystery shopping and work from home classes and feel totally prepared to get started. The information she provided about scams alone was worth the price of admission! She was clear, concise, enthusiastic, engaging, personable, professional, and was genuine in her interaction. The books she provided were well organized, and I can't wait to get started!

—Anonymous student review through Shoreline Community College

Bethany is truly the most knowledgeable person I know. When I needed extra money while trying to start my business, she taught me creative ways to earn an income. I continue to e-mail her new opportunities I see on Craigslist, and she always knows which ones are legit and which ones are scams. Her breadth of knowledge does not stop there, she also helps my new business with social media and keeps me updated on the newest Twitter rules and standards and ways to pimp out my Facebook fan page! She is truly a maven and a godsend to my business.

—Shalonne Foster (**www.fashionnetworkseattle.com**)

Bethany did a fabulous job of introducing us to mystery shopping! I had no idea it could be so involved and so much FUN. I can hardly wait to get started. Her genuine enthusiasm and knowledge of the subject was contagious. I look forward to learning more about other ways to make extra income in the future.

—Anonymous student review through Troy Continuing Education

Bethany is a good friend and mentor for me and my husband. Her wealth of knowledge and advice is drawn from her wide range of life experiences and business pursuits. She has a bounty to offer anyone from any walk of life. I have used her mystery shopping CD-ROM and materials to jumpstart my own mystery shopping pursuits, and the materials are not only clear and easy to follow but also humorous and entertaining. She presents the information sequentially and points out the possible pitfalls and scams to look for in the realm of mystery shopping. And the advice does not stop there - at any point, contact Bethany with any questions or concerns, and she will get back to you! This woman is successful, savvy, and most of all, sweet!

—Christine Kaputsky-Moore, Ian Tadashi-Moore (**www.iantm.com**)

Bethany makes working from home and Mystery Shopping sound like a real adventure! Her energy and enthusiasm throughout our class was contagious. I was really impressed with the book provided. It was comprehensive and laid out in a very organized manner. The class was well worth its value, and had much more information than I was expecting.

—Anonymous student review from Farmington Community Education

When I was looking to supplement my income, I turned to Bethany's "Become a Mystery Shopper" program. Within days I was accepting and completing assignments like a pro. The information she provided was clear, concise, and really helped me avoid the pitfalls and scams. Bethany has also been an invaluable resource in helping me streamline my business practices. Her knowledge of all things Internet has propelled me to a level of success I never knew possible! Any time I have questions regarding scams, marketing and social media, she is the first on my list to contact. Actually, she is the only person I would trust in giving me the whole picture about home based jobs, Internet marketing, social media practices, and scams.

—Jen Davidson (Jen Davidson Photography)

I Got Scammed So You Don't Have To!

How to Find Legitimate Work-at-Home, and Random Jobs in a Scamming Economy

Bethany Mooradian

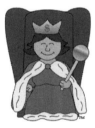

Moreradiant Publishing

I Got Scammed So You Don't Have To: How to Find Legitimate Work-at-Home, and Random Jobs in a Scamming Economy

ISBN13: **978-0-9802296-4-6**

Published by Moreradiant Publishing
Printed in the United States of America

Contents

Preface to the 2012 Edition

Even though I had published a book before, I really had no intention to write *I Got Scammed So You Don't Have To.*

In 2009, I had just been laid off from a steady consulting gig. I had lived the "random job" lifestyle for years, but I had grown accustomed to a fairly consistent paycheck (a novelty to me) and had let many of my other income streams dry up. It was a shock to the system once the gig was over as I had to rely on my savings and figure out my next step.

My varied background was both a blessing and a curse. The skills I had acquired over the years allowed me many different options, but at the same time, employers weren't hiring much in the down economy. And they especially weren't going to hire someone who was so vocal about her distaste for jobs in general. Think about it: would *you* hire a self-proclaimed "Queen of the Random Job" whose claim to fame was that she had never held a traditional 9 to 5 job for longer than nine months? Now that employers relied on Internet searches for a quick background check on potential employees...I was toast. There was just too much information about me out there.

I wasn't sure what direction to go in. I could make myself un-Googlable, and try the normal-job route. But deep down, I knew it wouldn't last. For the short-term, I was returning to random jobs just so I could eat, but it wasn't exactly sustainable as a true career path. At some point you get burned out from juggling so much. I could start my own business again...but doing what?

Since I couldn't answer my own question, I started attending every small business networking meeting I could find, in hopes of getting ideas. At least I could connect with other people with similar ideals who understood the entrepreneurial mindset. The two-minute introductions were always a little unnerving for me, though. People would stand up and proudly discuss their business, their ideal customer, and what they were looking for. When it came time for my turn, I tried to embrace my uncertainty. I stood up over and over again telling hundreds of people that I didn't know what I did and I had no clue as to what business I was in. I named off a lot of skills and jobs I had in the past and I ended my introductions with, "You tell me...what do I do?"

Surprisingly, the response was always positive. Many people sought me out after each event to talk to me about my background. They offered suggestions like starting my own job-placement agency, or resume help, or website design. Many approached me seeking advice with how they could earn extra income because their own business wasn't bringing in enough, but they couldn't get a job either. From those meetings and that feedback, I was able to figure out what I didn't want and what appealed to me. My business was re-born and this book was created.

I wish I could say it was an easy road to getting published, getting the book out there, and re-doing my business to meet your needs as well as my interests. But, it has always been a bit of a balancing act. Living off of random sources of income is no easy feat. Trying to live off of random sources of income while building a business is nearly impossible. But, whatever hardships I've had to endure to get this book into your hands is completely worth it, if somehow it provides you with ideas and resources to help you out.

This edition includes updates to nearly every single chapter, including company websites, resources, as well as 20 new direct sales businesses. Since the Internet changes on an hourly basis, I also encourage you to ask questions through my Website, Twitter, and Facebook pages. There, you'll find a supportive community of people who have similar interests in finding random ways to make extra money. It's a great way to learn from other people's experiences.

I am forever thankful to my family, my friends, my random employers, the entrepreneurs of Biznik and Meetup, my loyal readers, students, and raving fans, as well as those who challenge me to be better, for helping me realize my purpose of service to those looking to find a better way beyond the nine to five.

I hope this book provides even more reassurance that it's possible to live outside of the cubicle!

Bethany Mooradian
www.QueenoftheRandomJob.com
www.BuzzyRecommends.com
www.QueenBuzzy.com/Twitter
www.QueenBuzzy.com/Facebook
www.QueenBuzzy.com/YouTube

Introduction

In 1996, my 91-year-old grandfather passed away. I was 20, working and going to college in Detroit, and preparing to move across the country to Seattle. My sister was 23 and living in Memphis. His death had a significant impact on us both, and I remember how heartbroken my sister was, dissolving into tears because she couldn't get time off of work to go to the funeral. The job she had wasn't on a career path, it was a bookseller position at a regional chain, and I told her I thought she should quit. She said she simply couldn't. Jobs were hard to come by, and she was barely making ends meet as it was. I know it was a difficult decision for her, and while I supported her, it was hard for me to understand.

That moment had a profound effect on me. I vowed to never be in a position where a company held so much power over my life. If I was working, I wanted it to be flexible. I wanted to be able to take time off when I needed to, travel when I wanted to, and have the knowledge that no matter what, I was living a life that I created on my terms, rather than by someone else's schedule.

Of course, it is never as easy as it sounds. There have been times where I have wondered where my next paycheck was coming from, when I have been scammed out of money because I didn't see (or want to see) the signs, and when I just wanted to give up because the learning curve was so steep.

But every time I enter into the "real job" market, I come across a philosophy of living that just doesn't make sense to me. I see parents missing significant events in their children's lives, I see young professionals in cutthroat competition to get ahead, and blowing their money on happy hour just to decompress from a stressful day. I see the older generation getting downsized, retirement funds cut, and where they once thought their company would take care of them, realize now that they must continue working for the rest of their lives.

Even with these issues, I'm not against having a job per se; many people love working for others and achieve great success within their fields. Not everyone is an entrepreneur, and I understand that. It takes a certain amount of thick skin, passion and drive to create a company, or follow a business plan to completion. It is a fallacy, however, to think that the business you work at today will be around tomorrow, much less five or ten years from now. Even if it is, there is no guarantee that you won't be made redundant or downsized in some manner, and it is imperative to develop many income streams in case something falls through. At the very least, you need to educate yourself on how to identify scams and find legitimate opportunities out there while you're finding your passion.

How I Got Here

I will admit that I have not always practiced what I preach, and I have paid the price. Although the longest I have ever had a typical W-2 job was for nine months, I did have a steady consulting gig for nearly three years. The owner and I had an agreement that I would forego my other work and focus solely on her business. In exchange, I was paid handsomely.

The lure of a steady paycheck is seductive. I let many of my other income streams dry up because this company was taking care of my needs, and eating up most of my time. I got very comfortable. I was able to purchase a home, pay down debt, and then all of a sudden, the owner let me know that my services were no longer needed.

All at once, my main source of income disappeared. I had a few other things going at the time, but since all of my energy went into this company, most of them had laid dormant for years. To make matters worse, I was an independent contractor so I did not qualify for unemployment. Suddenly, I was forced to rely on my savings while I attempted to get a "real" job. I thought that was the only way I'd be able to afford my mortgage and expenses. It proved to be very difficult since not many people were hiring, and there were literally hundreds of applicants for any one position.

As time went on, my savings started drying up, and I decided to revert back to my former life as a "jack of all trades," thinking it would be just as challenging as finding a "real job." What I found was a pleasant surprise:

There were still a ton of mystery shopping assignments available. Focus groups and surveys were still in need of participants. Businesses were still in need of virtual assistants. Selling on eBay and Amazon was just as easy as I remembered it. Finding random sources of income had become a breeze with sites like Craigslist, Elance, and Guru. Of course, there were plenty of new scams out there to learn about, but with my 10+ years of experience, it was easy to see what was legitimate.

It was a huge relief. I knew that I could make my ends meet and get by while I tried to figure out my next move. Not knowing if I'd go back to pursuing by own business full time, or look for a steady job and do my own stuff on the side, I at least had the security of knowing I could get food on the table and keep a roof over my head while I figured it out.

My Ultimate Goal for You

My purpose for this book is to help you learn from my experiences, and educate you on what is real and what is not. Whether you're looking for extra income to get out of debt, save for college, plan for a vacation, or because you need something to help you get food on the table NOW, there are resources and tips to help you on your path.

The majority of e-mail I get at **QueenoftheRandomJob.com** asks "Is this a real job?" and so the first part of this book deals heavily with scams. You will learn how to decipher what you see, marketing techniques of scammers, how to track IP addresses and e-mails, as well as a lot of common scams out there.

The second and third parts of this book deal with making money! I'll go through various resources to sell your wares, trade your stuff, make money with various Websites and resources, as well as provide a host of companies that hire independent contractors that work from home, or have flexible hours.

The fourth part of this book deals with creating your own business. While a "job" is great, I truly believe that we can no longer rely on our employers to take care of us throughout the years. You'll learn about residual income, marketing and small business resources.

What This Book Isn't

When I started telling my friends and family that I was writing a book about finding legitimate work from home jobs and avoiding scams, I was met with skepticism. I was asked on more than one occasion, "How can you write a book about getting a job, when you can't find one yourself?" And, well, that's true. For some reason, after getting laid off from my consulting gig, I have had a devil of a time trying to find a "real job" so I certainly can't give any advice on that subject.

Unfortunately (or fortunately, depending on the perspective), the only jobs I have been able to get are the ones that I know are out there: the weird, random ways of making money. I am, in essence, my own best poster child, because I have yet to get a "real job" and I've had to rely on the resources that I've accumulated to make money, get food in my belly, and keep a roof over my head.

The Inevitable Disclaimers

It amazes me how much some people prefer to place blame on others rather than take responsibilities for their own actions and shortcomings. Because of this (and at the advice of legal counsel), I provide the following disclaimers:

1. I try my hardest to keep up with companies, trends, and of course, contact information of the companies and resources I discuss in this book. I can't guarantee that everything will be as up to date and accurate as it was the day that I wrote this version. The Internet moves at a speed faster than time itself, and information can change quickly. You can sign up for my newsletter at **www.QueenoftheRandomJob.com** for regular updates regarding scams and random sources of income. But, don't forget to use some common sense, do a little research on your own, and remember that if you don't like the job you end up with, it's up to you to change it!

2. I cannot guarantee that you'll get a job with any one company or in any industry that you learn about throughout the course of this book. It is up to you to develop the skills and talents needed, as well as conduct yourself in a professional manner throughout the hiring and employment process. I am not a recruiter; I simply provide information and resources to help you get started. I make no guarantees on income or hiring expectations.

3. If you do decide to go into business for yourself, be smart about it. I have failed in many businesses simply by not planning and thinking ahead. Desperation is never good for cash flow. Sit down, learn your local laws and regulations, and meet with consultants and advisors. As entrepreneurs, we're always eager to get started NOW, but take the time to think your business plan through so you don't fail right out of the gate.

Let's be clear: This book is not going to help you tweak your resume, discover your passion, or land the perfect job with a company that pays benefits, insurance, and two weeks' vacation. What it WILL do is teach you what to look for in finding legitimate work in the form of home businesses, work at home gigs, or independent contractor opportunities, and help you identify the factors that make up scams.

The types of jobs within these pages are not the ones that are going to make you millions unless that's what you want. While I see them as way to supplement income, or bridge the gap to more lucrative endeavors, I certainly am not one to put limits on what you can and cannot do.

There are plenty of people who make a full time income by being a virtual assistant, or by running an eBay business out of their home. My goal is to inform you of the opportunities that exist; what you do with this information is completely up to you! Many people end up realizing that a traditional job just doesn't suit their needs or goals once they know what else is out there.

After all, lot of life happens from 9 a.m. to 5 p.m. Do you really want to spend that time in a cubicle?

Part I

Techniques of Scammers and Common Scams

Chapter 1
The Psychology of Scamming

Scammers impress me greatly. They are quintessential salesmen and master magicians: convincing you to do things and believe words with little to no proof of reliability, legitimacy, or results. I honestly believe if scammers spent half of their energy in legitimate fields of industry, they would produce positive results for the good of society. Unfortunately, they're only in it for the quick buck, and possibly a high that comes with having power over desperate people, which means you have to go through life with your eyes wide open.

Although I am generally a very trusting person, I've been fortunate to have had experiences that helped me in discovering scams and seeing through hype:

The first was an assignment that I had in elementary school, where we had to watch an hour of TV each day for a week, write down all of the commercials we saw, and identify the words within the commercials to determine who the target audience was. This exercise was brilliant on so many levels.

Of course, as a kid, it was just really cool to tell my parents I *had* to watch TV for my homework. But the conversation that it sparked afterwards was very enlightening, even to my naïve nine-year-old mind. I remember debating with my classmates about various ads, especially the ones that ran on Saturday morning, figuring out how companies would make us want to buy the products through various words, colors, characters, and phrases.

The teacher made us think about why companies were gearing commercials to children instead of adults since we didn't have jobs or money. And it made us realize the power we had in influencing our parents, and how manipulative companies could be to make us want things that we didn't really need. I remember being a bit angry, actually, thinking that corporations were trying to use us kids to get to our parents, just because we were young and didn't know any better.

And, frankly, part of me believes this is why I have never been into designer labels, high fashion style, or anything that is considered "hip." I'm very unhip. I'm first to admit it, and primarily I think it's because I just don't buy into marketing techniques since I'm hyperaware of manipulation.

Advice from my father has also helped me to maintain a healthy dose of skepticism throughout my life. My dad was a newspaper reporter and editor for over 40 years before he retired to write his memoir, *The Repatriate* (**www.TheRepatriate.com**), and he instilled a realistic fear in both my sister and me by recounting events that he had to report on. But even more so than learning about fire safety, drugs, guns, speeding, and criminals, were the words that always hung in the air, "Consider the Source." Even though my father worked for the newspapers, he told me that the media always got the story wrong. Everything was always slanted, mostly by accident, but it could be done deliberately just to make for a better story.

To this day, no matter what anyone tells me, I always consider the source, and take everything with a grain of salt. Unless I hear from Bill Gates himself that he's giving people who e-mail everyone they know $1,000, I'm going to assume that it's some kind of hoax.

Just because my brain has been embedded with these lessons does not mean that I'm above falling for stupid scams. I've been scammed plenty of times in a variety of ways that have hurt both my wallet and my ego. Luckily, I'm a quick learner, and as it stands now I actually look for new scams so I can offer myself up as a potential victim to see how each one works!

Ultimately, there are just a few reasons why scammers scam:

- They want your money.
- They want your information (Social Security Number, credit card info, bank account info, etc.).
- They want to use you to get other people's money or information.
- They can get away with it.

It seems simple and logical doesn't it? But knowing this information can make you very powerful when looking at opportunities online. For example:

- If a company asks you for your credit card info, it should set off a red flag that it's not legit.
- If a company asks for your social security number and bank account info, it should set off a red flag.
- If a company says that you are acting as a payment processor and you'll be writing checks to other employees, or dealing with other people's credit card numbers and social security numbers, be wary.
- If a company is located overseas, or even out of your state/province, and therefore not bound by local laws, it should set off a red flag.

I'm not saying that a company is a scammer if any one of these items applies. After all, it could need your routing information for direct deposits of your paycheck. It could need you to run company reports for their other employees. It *could* need a lot of things that may make it seem like a scam, when in actuality, it isn't. But if any of these apply, you *need* to do your due diligence, research it further, and make sure that it is on the up and up.

Of course just knowing this information doesn't really protect you from their carefully crafted ads and Websites. Because we are human and generally make decisions based on emotion not logic, scammers can be successful in conning you because:

- You think it's a great deal.
- You don't look close enough (or want to look close enough) to see the fraud.
- You're desperate and think they're your only option.

And all of these can be summed up with one simple fact:

You WANT to believe it's true.

It's this "want" that gets us into trouble. We want to believe it's true because we need the job, we need the money, and we need the freedom of working from home or the flexibility in hours. We want to believe, and so we overlook parts of the ad or post or Website that set off the red flags to take away our belief.

Any great scammer will tell you that lies are most effective when there is an inkling of truth in them. Heck, any seven-year-old kid who is trying to get away with something knows that too!

Many scam ads out there will rely on this element of your psyche to lure you in. Throughout the ad, you might see:

- Something you know to be true.
- Something that is easy to assume to be true.
- Something that you're unfamiliar with.
- Compelling beliefs that other people have had success.

So just remember, scammers can get away with scamming because each scam contains a little nugget of truth.

Consider these scenarios:

- Medical Billing from home is a legitimate way to make extra money. You do need specific training and specific materials. Scammers will charge you for these things, but not deliver. (If medical billing/transcription interests you, visit **ahdionline.org** for legitimate training possibilities)
- Doing online surveys is another way to make extra money. Most companies set a payment threshold for $100 so they don't have to send $2 checks. The real companies will pay you, but scammers will wait until you reach about $75 and stop sending you surveys to complete! (Look for legitimate survey companies in Part II.)
- Mystery Shopping is a wonderful way to make extra money by evaluating customer service at a variety of establishments. Check-cashing businesses as well as banks do get evaluated. Scammers take advantage of this by asking you to cash a (fake) check and wire back the difference to someone overseas. Several weeks later you'll find that the check was fake and be out the money. Mystery Shopping is my favorite random job, and we'll go into some details about how to get started in Part III.)

Because your emotional mind will see the 'part-truth' of the scam, your rational mind may choose to take a backseat. Couple that with compelling stories from other people who have had success with the company, and you're ready to fall for the scam, hook, line, and sinker!

We'll talk more about specific marketing techniques and examples of scams from my own life and experiences in later chapters. For now, just remember that scammers are only as successful as you allow them to be.

Chapter 2
Jobs versus Opportunities

I get a lot of e-mail from people telling me that too many companies ask them to pay fees of some sort when they're looking for jobs. They go on and on about how they're being scammed because they don't want to pay any money to work for someone.

Frankly, I think calling "scam" at every corner shows a lack of logic and deductive reasoning skills. The people who are so quick to cry foul at any given moment really do so because they want to cover up for their own lack of skills or research. In our victim-mentality culture, it seems like no one wants to take responsibility for their actions, or do the work needed to succeed. Especially in business! This is why so many opportunities out there are classified as scams when really, they're not—99.9% of the time I can almost guarantee that the person who ventured into it simply didn't do the research or follow the directions to make it work for them.

Now, I know I'm a little more sensitive to it than most. After all, I do work in the work-at-home realm, and we're ripe with *real* scammers. It tends to irk me when I see legitimate companies getting a bad rap. To date, I have not yet been called a scam or fraud, but I'm sure it's just a matter of time. I'm simply not famous enough yet. Tony Robbins, Oprah, Bill Gates, and even Mother Teresa and Gandhi have all been called scams and frauds. Seriously! Search for any name, any business, and you're bound to find a few disgruntled people who are more than happy to share with the world how they have been deceived.

If you feel like you're being scammed because someone wants you to purchase training, get a background check or buy into a business, keep in mind that these types of offers aren't necessarily scams. The most important thing is to do extensive research on the company so you know why fees are involved.

It is OK to spend money on:

- Training
- Materials, Technology or Programs
- Information
- Background check/credit check

It is *NOT* OK to spend money:

- If the "employer" guarantees employment
- On job-placement agencies
- If you don't thoroughly do your research on the company and individuals before signing up!

Remember, sometimes the person running a "work at home" job ad wants to sell you on an **opportunity**, as opposed to a **job**. There is a big difference, and it's important that you know the distinction before you go declaring SCAM to every ad and website.

Jobs consist of work that you do to help an employer reach their goals.
Jobs may pay you per hour or per assignment.
Jobs may classify you as an employee or an independent contractor.
Jobs may allow you to work from home or at a specific location.

Examples of jobs (either of the "employee" or "independent contractor" variety): Merchandising, virtual assisting, babysitting online tutoring, phone book delivery, and preparing taxes.

Pros of having a JOB	**Cons of having a JOB**
You are not responsible for the overall health of the business.	Someone else determines your hourly worth.
Can be consistent income.	The company could go under, merge, or downsize you at any time.
Can come with benefits.	Flexibility of hours is limited.
May provide you with a sense of security in having a steady paycheck.	Someone is constantly evaluating your performance.

Opportunities mean that you run your own business.
Opportunities require training in the industry.
Opportunities require that you find your own customers.
Opportunities may require a financial investment.
Opportunities usually pay on a commission basis.
Opportunities may have a residual aspect to your compensation.

Examples of opportunities: Running a Subway™ franchise, medical transcription where you find your own clients, selling Avon, Tupperware, etc., affiliate programs (selling on eBay™ or Amazon™), and running a website with ads on it.

Pros of having an Opportunity	Cons of having an Opportunity
Unlimited income potential.	Most small business owners work much more than a 40-hour week, especially in the beginning.
You are your own boss and make your own hours.	You are responsible for keeping track of your money and taxes and abiding by all laws.
You can hire other people to do the grunt work.	You may not be successful.
You can structure your business to run automatically, so that you make money 24 hours a day.	Working on your own business is very solitary. You won't have coworkers to chat with.
You receive a ton of tax deductions.	You will have a learning curve (the products, the company, marketing, and advertising). There is always something new to learn to help your business grow, and you will always have to invest money and time into your business.

When you're looking at ads online, or happen upon a website that has job listings, keep these things in mind as you scrutinize the ads. Use deductive reasoning and do your research on the company and job offer. Before you toss anything aside as a scam, just ask yourself: "Is this a JOB or an OPPORTUNITY?" You might find the perfect opportunity that fulfills you more than any job could.

Chapter 3
MLM and Direct Sales
Three Case Studies

I love MLM. I know you're probably shocked because I seem like such an intelligent person, but it's true. I love MLM, and I think the misconceptions of the industry need to be addressed. Let's face it, you're going to encounter several MLMs on your job hunt and if you're tempted to join one, you need to know how to weed out the junk from the gems.

You probably have already had an experience with MLM, network marketing, or direct sales. Perhaps your uncle was selling Amway, maybe your neighbor threw Tupperware parties—maybe you were invited to one of those horribly cheesy seminars at the local Hilton Hotel, or maybe you've been "in" a company and it just left a bad taste in your mouth, or maybe you were wildly successful, in which case, I'm wondering why you're reading this book. But I digress . . .

For those of you not familiar with the concept, MLM is short for "Multi-Level Marketing", in which there are different ways (or levels) of making money. The terms *MLM, network marketing,* and *direct sales* are interchangeable. All this really means is that products are sold directly to the consumer (generally with no middleman or retail outlet) and that there is a commission component that allows a distributor to recruit others and earn additional income off of their sales as well. Most people think of MLM as a pyramid scheme because you are considered to be the top of your pyramid, and your sales force below you completes the triangle.

If you think about it, a pyramid is how most companies are organized. Most corporations have the CEO (the "top" of the pyramid) and then there is upper management, middle management, lower management, and finally, the humble worker. The only difference is that with MLMs you, as a humble worker, get to make money not only off of the sales of products, but also any other humble worker that works with you. As you progress up the management chain you'll earn commissions off of all of the humble workers who you mentor to follow the system. Personally, I would rather work with a group of people where our earnings are set not only on what we produce, but through the work of others as well. It gives more of a "we're all in this together" sense of community. In traditional employment, a manager fires the humble worker when they're not producing, or even just because they need to make cuts. In MLMs, a "manager" will mentor the humble worker to success so that they can also reap the benefits from the humble worker's work.

Because there is an established system to follow with products and services in place, I tend to think of MLM as "mini-franchising." It's very similar to opening a McDonald's or Subway but without the hefty franchise fee. Most MLM start-up costs are between $50 and $500 (compared to $300,000 for a fast-food joint, it's not a bad deal). If you're looking to follow a pre-established system, and you want some freedom of working for yourself, MLM companies are pretty decent options.

However, the biggest problem with MLMs is the manner in which they are pitched. People tend to forget that running a business requires time and effort. You're still going to have to market and advertise your products. If you recruit others, you're going to have to train and support them. Too many people are sold on MLMs from one over-hyped meeting that promises them the world, and then they get jaded when it all comes crashing down.

Case Study #1: Rainbow Cleaning System

My first experience with direct sales was with the Rainbow vacuum cleaner. (Of course, they'd be really annoyed that I called it a vacuum cleaner, since it uses water instead of filters so it's not a vacuum, because it doesn't suck—pun is totally intended.) I found out about the Rainbow because I answered an employment advertisement. I went to a group interview where they then demonstrated the joys and splendors of Rainbow. And, man, I was hooked. The concept totally made sense, and although the price tag was insane (around $2,000 at the time), the commission structure was amazing (around $300 per sale, and $100 per sale from my down-line) and I really liked the product. At the time, I thought I could just sell one per week and I'd be all set.

I had no sales experience whatsoever. The training was pretty lax; all they asked was that I "demonstrate" the product to my friends and get referrals. Of course, they didn't realize that I was a broke puppeteer at the time, and being in my early 20s, most of my friends were broke artists as well, but I pressed on.

After doing about 10 demonstrations with no sales, the owner of my branch took me under his wing. He gave me leads, took me on his sales calls, gave me books to read, coached me on cold-calling and recruiting, and held small classes on sales techniques. It really was a great education, but I came to realize that I really had no desire to sell $2,000 vacuum cleaners, no matter how effective they were.

Was I scammed? I don't think so. I was paid "per appointment" up to 15 appointments made, (plus commission on any sales) and afterwards was clearly told that the compensation was commission only. I really believed in the product but couldn't find the right people to sell it to. I didn't like the way that leads were gathered, (forcing people to give leads during the demonstration, or going door-to-door offering free vacations), but that's the way the company was set up. There are a lot of business practices that I don't believe in (like those companies who use sweatshops), but that just means that I don't do business with, or work for, those companies. Just because we have different ideas on how to do business doesn't mean that I was scammed.

Case Study #2: Link 2 Be Free/Link 2 the Future

My second experience with MLM was with a company called Link 2 Be Free (it then became Link 2 the Future, and then it closed!). It was an online business that had products to sell like vitamins, health care, legal services, etc, as well as a shopping mall where people could earn commissions off of purchases through large name retailers like Best Buy, 1800 Flowers, and others.

I didn't seek Link 2 Be Free out—it actually found me. I had placed an ad in the local paper selling my book on Mystery

Shopping (this was in 2002, when the Internet wasn't as nearly prolific as it is today). One of the representatives, Fred, contacted me, because he thought my ad was about shopping through Link. He had never heard of mystery shopping before. So, I went to his group meeting, held at an office park (the company owners had day jobs as engineers), and saw the presentation. To be honest, the commissions were paltry, just a few cents or dollars for each transaction. Of course, the power was in finding people to shop through your store, so it wasn't just your own sales earning your commission, and finding people who wanted to be store owners as well. None of that really appealed to me, but what drew me in was that the $200 yearly fee included a fully customizable website. I knew I needed a website to sell my Mystery Shopping book, so I was pretty much sold.

I was in Link for about a year, and yes, I did actually make money—not at much as I put into it, of course. There were internal issues with the company and it folded. It's a shame too, because the concept was very simple: shop through your own affiliate programs and earn commissions. I understand it now more than I did then, just because affiliate programs are so commonplace now (they're explored later in this book), but was I scammed? Not really. Granted, I don't know what happened behind closed doors to make them fold, but I do know now that MLMs with less than a five-year history are risky. I still consider it a good learning experience especially since I have friends from Link that are still in my life today, and I learned a lot about Internet marketing, affiliate programs, and coding HTML.

Case Study #3: Global Domains International (GDI)

My third adventure in MLM was with Global Domains International (GDI). It owns the .ws extension, and its product is a website. I needed websites, they were only $10/month, and I was sold. I would earn $1 per month off of everyone I put in my downline, and it was really easy for me to find people, since everyone needs a website nowadays.

I even ended making a little bit of money! Not a lot, because I soon realized that the websites were only limited to five pages each

(I need much more) and that they weren't fully customizable as advertised (you could pick themes and move things around, but you couldn't create your own page from scratch). The .ws domain is considered spam since so many people are pitching the business, so most of my e-mails were never delivered (or were blocked, or whatever), and I knew I'd have to quit. I couldn't promote a product that I couldn't use, even though it was the simplest and most profitable concept out there. A few of my down-line are still in it, and are having success, but for me, it didn't work.

Did GDI scam me? Again, I don't think so. We had different ideas of what "fully customizable," meant. I thought I could live with a five-page website, when in actuality, I really couldn't. I still think it's a great concept, but for people who are serious about e-commerce, having a .ws domain will most likely hinder, not help, their business.

Conclusion

It is my opinion that people feel scammed by MLMs because they don't take the time to research the company and what is needed to run a business. They're taken in by the hype and the blatant appeals to materialism and greed. They want the large homes and nice cars, and think it's attainable if they just put two or three or ten people below them. Not a thought is given to marketing the products or even trying the products to see if they're remotely decent. People want to believe in instant wealth so badly that they'll gladly buy tapes and CDs and books and anything that the company throws at them instead of a basic business, marketing, or sales course.

On your job hunt, you will encounter MLMs. Don't feel bad if one of them catches your eye—just be realistic about what you'll need to do, and follow these simple steps before you join:

1. Find out how long the company has been in business, and if the founders have any sketchy legal matters in their past. If the company has been around less than 3 to 5 years, don't bother. They're too new to know what they're doing.
2. Research the company for 6 to 9 months before joining. Attend all the meetings and conference calls that you can.

Don't be swayed by people telling you that you need to get in "now." Every time I read "The Tortoise and The Hare," the tortoise always wins. Take your time. You wouldn't open up any brick and mortar business without doing your research, would you?

3. Follow the person who would be putting you in, as well as their leaders to determine what kind of support and training you'd be getting. Do you trust them? Do you like them?
4. Find someone who has been in the business for at least three years and has been successful at it. Pick their brain and see if what they did is duplicable.
5. Determine if the compensation is worth it to you. Can you make income just by selling products? Most companies will make it very worthwhile to have distributors under you, but if you have to spend your time convincing people to join the business instead of selling your products then you're doomed to fail. Not everyone is an entrepreneur, but everyone is a consumer. Make sure your "consumer compensation" is worth your time.
6. What do you get for your start-up fees? What ongoing or renewing fees are there? Can the compensation plan and all fees be explained in less than 60 seconds?
7. Try the products. Do you like them?

If the idea of MLM intrigues you, check out Part IV to see a list of companies to get started with.

Chapter 4
Deciphering Affiliate Programs

Affiliate programs are more likely to be considered scams than any other opportunity out there. This is in part due to marketing techniques that make affiliate programs seem like legitimate job offers, when really they are just business opportunities. We'll discuss these techniques in an upcoming chapter, but for now, let's delve into the nitty-gritty of affiliate programs.

The gist of an affiliate program is this: A vendor (could also be called an advertiser) has a product or service to sell. An affiliate (could also be called a publisher) has (or is willing to get) customers who are interested in the product or service. Should activity result from the affiliate's efforts (could be a sale, sign-up, or a click on a website), the Vendor will pay the Affiliate commission based on the activity.

If you're lucky, some affiliate programs will allow affiliates to earn commission off of sub-affiliates. This means that if someone is interested in being an affiliate through a specified vendor, and they sign up through you, you will earn commission off of their sales as well, or at least get a little bonus with the affiliate signs up: creating even more residual income for you!

Many companies that you already know and love have affiliate programs: Amazon.com, eBay.com, 1-800 Flowers, Home Shopping Network, Home Depot, Yahoo, Google, Sears, Walgreens—the list goes on and on.

Each affiliate program is different. The commission rates vary, the payment schedules vary, the payout rates vary, the rules in which vendors will accept affiliates will vary, and the conditions in which affiliates are allowed to advertise will vary. Each one is unique in details but common in the concept.

Affiliate programs are possible through the power of tracking technology. Everything is done online and through the Web. When you sign up to be an affiliate, you'll receive a unique ID and link that ties the activity (sale, signup, or click) to your account. When you advertise that link (through your own site, on message boards, on job boards, or in the off-line world) and people visit it, you'll be able to see your results: sales, clicks, commissions, etc. through your affiliate account.

You can make legitimate income with affiliate programs! You do have to learn a bit about affiliate marketing, Internet marketing, and other fun Web-stuff to get started, but once you do, you certainly have the ability to create a very good source of income.

Affiliate programs get a bad rap when they seemingly deceive the customer. For example, you might see a job post on Craigslist about making money by taking online surveys. You answer the ad, and get a response back about purchasing a program or list of companies that will pay you to take surveys from home. You feel deceived because you thought you were answering an ad for a legitimate company, and instead this "scammer" wants you to pay money.

Again, they're not scamming you. They're selling a product that gives you the information that you want, and in turn, they get commission. Granted, they advertised in the wrong section. But they're not necessarily scamming you.

Another example would be when you're searching Google for "home-based businesses" and get a plethora of results, half of which want you to pay for listings or information. You feel scammed because you expected to get something else, and instead feel forced to pay for information you wanted for free.

Are you seeing a common thread here? Instead of feeling scammed, letting yourself get frustrated and all worked up that you can't trust anything you see online, try changing your perception! Realize that there are affiliate programs out there, there are people who are going to try and sell you stuff that you may or may not benefit from, and it's really just a matter of knowing what you're looking at to make an informed decision.

Full disclaimer: I have purchased products through affiliate programs, both that I have loved, and that have done nothing for me, AND I sell my products through affiliate programs. As a vendor, I find that it increases my sales force one hundred-fold, I don't have to concentrate so much on marketing, and I can spend my time supporting my customers, rather than advertising my products. It's a win-win-win for my affiliates, my customers, and myself.

How to Spot an Affiliate Program

It's really quite simple: look for the tracking ID! Remember that affiliate programs only work when tracking is in place so that the Vendor can appropriately credit the affiliate for delivering the sale. All you need to do is look for the tracking ID to determine whether the information you're looking at is for an affiliate program.

Smart affiliates will have a simple domain name for you to remember, and redirect that domain name to their affiliate link. This means the true URL may not appear in the browser address bar. Pay attention to the bottom of your browser screen when you're mousing over and clicking on links. There, you will see the true address that you're being redirected to, and any affiliate IDs.

For example, the website where I sell my mystery shopping training program is **www.ShopperTraining.com.** If an affiliate wanted to promote my program, and become my affiliate, after he signed up, he would receive its own link that looked like this:

www.shoppertraining.com/?hop=incognito5.

The tail end of that string, "incognito5" is the affiliate ID and lets me know who delivered the sale. You'll notice, if you go to that site (just open up a browser to copy and paste: **www.shoppertraining.com/ ?hop=incognito5**), the website is the same—it's not a separate site. The link just has extra coding so that tracking can occur.

Not all affiliate links look the same, but they all have the same concept. FYI, it is usually the string of numbers/letters/words after an "=" near an "id" or "hop" or "refid" or a "#" that shows what the affiliate ID is. This is just a general rule of thumb, however. Once you start getting used to seeing affiliate IDs, you'll get the hang of how the different codes work. Just keep in mind that when you mouse over the link, it will show you where the link is going and who the affiliate is. It really is just that simple!

Look at this example:

http://www.thisisafakesite.com/?gclid=CO-g76Wzyp0CFR4HagodMSHUsA

The string of numbers and letters after "gclid="(the underlined portion) is the tracking ID for this affiliate link.

http://www.thisisalsoafakesite.com/?cid=52085&kid=2150572358&fp=f

For this example, the first affiliate ID is "52085" and the second is "2150572358." (Both underlined in this example.) From these two IDs, we can gather that this company allows sub-affiliates. This means not only does an affiliate earn commission off of their own sales, but it can find others to sell the product and earn commission that way as well.

What Do I Do with This Information?

Now that you know what affiliate programs are and how to spot them, you'll be amazed at how many you encounter in your e-mail, online, and on message boards. Many of Google's search results on the right-hand side are affiliate programs!

Armed with this information, you now have the freedom to relax. Instead of worrying if something is a scam, you can say, "Oh, it's just another affiliate program. They're trying to sell me something." Who knows? If you actually like the product, you can turn around and become an affiliate yourself, making some money by selling it to other people.

As a side note, affiliate IDs are extremely powerful when tracking spammers, and those who send out porn to unwilling (or underage) recipients. Because affiliate IDs are necessary to see the real person behind the advertisements, police can use this information to find and prosecute those who are breaking CAN-SPAM laws.

For more information on how to make money with affiliate programs, see Part II.

Chapter 5
Behind the Scenes of Online Marketing

Online marketing is a fascinating topic that I could discuss for hours on end. Since hundreds of people have already written books, articles, and guides exploring the in-depth intricacies of the Internet marketing world, I don't really feel the need to address those issues here. If it's a topic that is of interest to you, I recommend you check out your local library for resources to help you get started.

For the purposes of this book, I'm really just going to focus on the basics: how you can gather information on a website owner, and identify marketing techniques while on the job hunt. Much like my elementary school teacher, I hope to open your eyes to blatant manipulation from an insider's point of view.

The Basics of Getting Online

Have you ever wondered what it meant to log on to the Internet? What kind of information about you is available to the public when you get online or send an e-mail? While I am far from being an expert about these things, here are some basic tidbits you need to know to thwart the bad guys and keep yourself safe.

What Is an IP address?

An Internet Protocol (IP) address is to your computer what your home address is to your house. It is an exclusive number that all information technology devices (routers, modems, etc.) use that identify them and allow them to talk to each other. Just like if someone did not have your correct home address, you would never receive your bills, pizza delivery, or a birthday card from Grandma. If you didn't have an assigned IP address, you would never be able to access information like your e-mail account, surf the Web, or send something over a shared network. IP addresses are a series of number separated by periods (for example: 255.543.5.1 or 41.255.255.253).

When the Internet first started, all sites were categorized by these IP addresses. As you can imagine, it was very hard to remember the proper sequence, so the Domain Name System (DNS) came into being. This allowed the assigning of a name to a particular IP address. After all, it was easier to remember **www.queenbuzzy.com** instead of 208.109.181.52, and it's easier to remember **info@queenbuzzy.com** rather than info@208.109.181.52. (You can find the IP address of a website by going to **http://www.selfseo.com/find_ip_address_of_a_Website.php.** Sometimes if you enter in the IP address into your browser, you'll be able to go directly to the site!)

IP addresses not only identify websites and e-mail addresses but also individual computers accessing the Internet. Yes, this can feel like a huge invasion of privacy, because in essence it means that the browsing you do can be identified by your IP address. It is highly doubtful that you are being monitored, however, so just relax. Think of it this way: Your computer has an IP address that dials through your Internet service provider's IP address which then contact's the IP address of the website you want to visit. Just like you have a phone number to call your Grandma's phone number so you two can chat and catch up on all the family gossip. And while the cops have the ability to eavesdrop on your phone conversation, it is highly unlikely to happen.

How Do I Trace an IP address?

There are a couple of great sites that will help you discover your IP address. The site **http://www.whatismyip.com/tools/ip-address-lookup.asp** will tell you the IP address of your computer. This number may change depending on the day and time that you use it. When we sign up for the Internet through a company, (Like Comcast, Century Link, SBC, etc.) it usually has a very large block of IP addresses available to its customers. Unless you specifically ask for a "static" IP address (meaning that it never changes), you'll be sharing various addresses with other customers. If Comcast had just one IP for everyone to dial through to reach the Internet, your connection would be reaaaaaally slow!

What Are Domain Extensions?

The domain extension is the last part of a website name. For example: **.com**, **.net**, **.org**, **.edu**, **.gov**, etc. Anyone can get a **.com**, (for 'company') **.net** ('network') or **.org** ('organization') extension, but only accredited schools can get a **.edu** extension, and only US government entities can register a **.gov**. If you visit websites or receive emails from sites ending in **.edu** or **.gov**, they're legit, and definitely not scammy.

Each country has its own extension as well. If you get an email from a **.de**,(Germany) **.fr**, (France) **.ru**, (Russia) **.jp**, (Japan) or **.ca** (Canada) domain, or visit a website with those extensions, keep in mind that you are dealing with people outside of the United States.

What Are E-mail Headers?

Most of us view compact e-mail headers when we read our e-mail. If you choose to view your "full" e-mail header, you will see a lot of technical jargon like this:

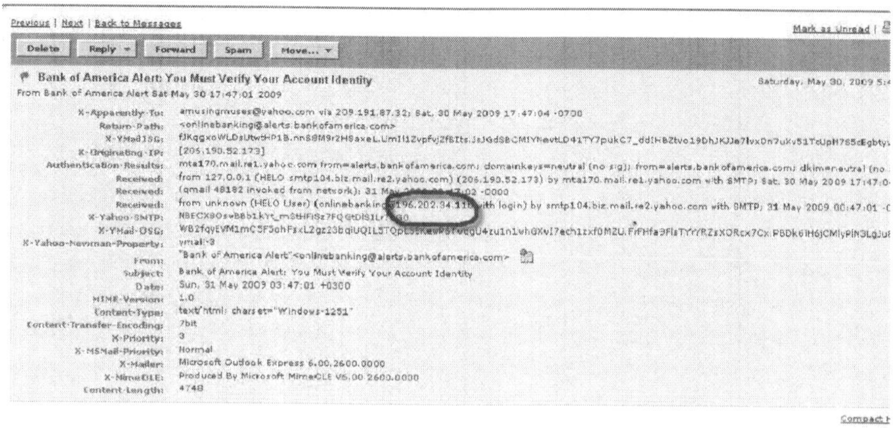

If you looked at the "received" paths, you'll see a lot of IP addresses. You can then trace those IP addresses to see where the e-mail came from. (The IP address 196.202.34.116 is circled above.)

How Do I View My Headers?

Each e-mail program is different. Check out the "help" section of your email provider's site and just search for "view full headers" to get information.

Can an E-mail Be Traced?

Well, yes and no. You can look in your e-mail headers to find the IP addresses. Usually there is more than one IP address, as they tend to get bounced around as they go from network to network to reach you. Once you find the IPs, you can go to **www.ARIN.net** and enter in the digits to see the company that owns it. Because a large Internet Service Provider may have a block of numbers, you probably won't be able to see the individual who used that IP address. Rather, the company would be listed. Tracing IPs is never an exact science, but at least you now have somewhere to start.

The Basics of Getting a Website

In order for a company to have a website, they have to register their domain name (for example, **www.bethanymooradian.com**) and host the pages somewhere. Some people choose to have their name and host at the same company, others choose to have them be separate.

According to the Internet Corporation for Assigned Names and Numbers (ICANN), every single website must have a legitimate owner and up-to-date contact information. Because of this, some website owners choose to go through a proxy so that their private information isn't viewed by the world. The contact information then becomes that of the proxy company, but the registration dates are still viewable and valid.

Why This Matters

You can research how long a company has been around by going to **www.whois.com** or **www.dnstools.com**. Type in its domain name, and you'll see how long its name has been registered, who is it registered to, and when it is set to expire. If the company hasn't been around for a long period of time, it might be a fly-by-night operation. Remember, even if it's a private registration, the listing will have registration date information.

If you ever choose to get your own website and register your domain, you have to provide your real address, e-mail, and phone number. Unless you choose a private registration, anyone can view this information. Spammers (and marketers) use these listings to send you notices to try and get you to switch hosts, domain registry companies, or just sell you stuff. Getting a private registration masks your information from the world, usually for just a few dollars per year.

Subdomains

A "domain" is a term for a website name, such as **www.queenoftherandomjob.com.** This is also called a Universal Resource Locater or URL and really just tells a Web browser where to go to get data related to that name. A subdomain is a part of the domain commonly used to assign a unique name to a service or area of the company. For example, I might have **www.joblistings.queenoftherandomjob.com** as a URL, where "joblistings" is the subdomain, and "queenoftherandomjob.com" is the main domain. Many companies have subdomains just to divide up their business for easy organization.

A very good example of this is Wikipedia, which uses subdomains to divide up its listings based on language: **http://en.wikipedia.org** is for English, **http://fr.wikipedia.org** is for French, etc.

Why This Matters

Scammers will try to deceive you through the power of subdomains. They could have a website like **www.paypal.thisisafakesite.com** where "paypal" is the subdomain of the main domain "thisisafakesite.com." If you're not paying attention, you might think that you're going to the PayPal site, when in reality, you're heading off to "thisisafakesite.com"

Same rules apply with e-mails! If you get an e-mail from: **info@usatoday.fictionalwebsite.com,** you aren't actually corresponding with someone at *USA Today* rather someone at **fictionalwebsite.com** thinks they're being pretty savvy.

Masking Links and URL Shorteners

Now that Twitter and Facebook are commonplace (I'm on them too: **www.queenbuzzy.com/twitter, www.queenbuzzy.com/facebook**), we all are trying to find ways to sum up the joy and excitement in our lives (like what we had for breakfast) in tidy little posts.

Twitter requires users to keep posts to 140 characters or less. If you can imagine trying to post a link to a website, especially one with a really long name (like "queenoftherandomjob.com" for example) a lot of those characters just get used up. Many people use URL shorteners like **www.tinyurl.com**, **www.bit.ly,** and **www.urltea.com** to shorten their very long URLs.

For example, the full link to a post on my blog would take up the majority of a Facebook or Twitter post character limit: **http://www.queenoftherandomjob.com/9-ways-so-turni-your-idea-into-multiple-income-sources.** But, if I just go to bit.ly and copy and paste the URL, I can shrink it to a very usable: **http://bit.ly/s51cfQ**. If you go to the bit.ly link, it's still the same post, just shortened and masked.

Bit.ly, Urltea.com and tinyurl.com aren't the only shorteners around, though. And many companies have taken to customizing their shortened links to build brand awareness. Can you guess what company this shortened URL is linking to? **http://amzn.to/hS9IGT** (Hint: it's Amazon.)

Affiliate marketers often mask their links as well since they don't want people to steal their affiliate commissions. For example, if an affiliate link is **http://www.shoppertraining.com/?hop=incognito5** and is plainly viewable for all to see, there is nothing stopping someone from signing up for the affiliate program themselves and replacing "incognito5" with their own affiliate ID, thereby stealing the commission.

Why This Matters

Scammers and spammers use these services too! They like to mask their links so you don't know where you're going on the Web. This can be dangerous because you might be heading to a site that downloads a virus, or you may inadvertently wind up somewhere you don't want to be. Before you click, consider the source. Remember that even friends get hacked, and their hacked accounts might send you something you don't want. If it feels fishy, you can visit **www.realurl.org** to get the *real* Web address before you visit. Just enter in the shortened URL and **www.realurl.org** will show you the actual website address, without your computer actually accessing the site. And remember, sometimes it is better not to click than to appease your curiosity.

Deconstructing Those One-Page Web Sites

If you've spent anytime whatsoever online, especially if you've been looking for ways to make money, I know you've encountered the really long, one-page website that just wants you to BUY NOW! It's slick and snazzy, and designed with very specific elements to make you interested in the product or service. I have been doing Internet marketing since 2003, and I don't know of one colleague who likes the endless one-page sales letter. As far as I can tell, we all hate it. However, for some reason, that obnoxiously long letter really works. It delivers results, and as long as we get sales, we're going to continue to use it and any other techniques available to us that help convert prospects to buyers.

Again, these are just techniques that marketers use. It does not necessarily mean that the website is a scam.

The Fake Countdown Clock

In order to get sales, sometimes you must present limited opportunity to create a sense of urgency to buy. This can be achieved with a "countdown" clock. Sometimes it's counting down

unshorten.me

the minutes or seconds left to get a product at a particular price. Other times it's counting down the number of products remaining. Regardless, if you let the timer run out, your world will not implode. The offer will still be there at the price listed, giving you another four, three, no, *two* more minutes to BUY NOW!

The Flog

A "flog" is simply a fake blog. The website is set up to look like a blog, it may even have links to a few other posts, and "comments" from others. Most likely, the comments are "disabled due to spam." You can tell it's fake, however, because the posts are all centered on a product, and all of the comments talk about how great the product is.

Fake News Headlines

Some websites are designed to look like online versions of newspapers. This is very prevalent in the health and beauty industry. There will be several different columns by various authors talking about the benefits of their products. At a casual glance, it really does look like a legitimate news source. But once you start reading, you'll see that all of the articles are geared towards the promotion of a select few products, and affiliate links abound. (News 6 Boston doesn't exist!)

"AS SEEN ON..."

The thing that irks me the most in Web marketing is the "As seen on" claim with a list of logos from trusted news sources that you recognize (like *USA Today*, NBC, *Redbook*). Those logos are simply that: just logos. There are no links to articles about the program or product on those sites, there are no interviews with the creator, and there is nothing to prove legitimacy. They're just there to build trust without substance. Many times, websites like these get brief mentions through various feeds of large well-known publications because a press release was submitted. But, most of the time, people who use this marketing technique are just liars.

Social Proof

Any Internet marketer will tell you that social proof is necessary when you need to sell something over the Web. At its basic level, "Social Proof" is just someone else giving their endorsement of the product or company. Ebay and Amazon use this very well with their ratings system. Marketers use this online by having testimonials. When you see others giving feedback about something you're interested in, you're more likely to buy—making marketers very happy!

Review Sites

Building on the Social Proof model, a style of sales website has popped up in recent times: the Review Site. On it, you have a trusted third-party source that is giving his unbiased reviews on various products and services. Usually the trusted source offers one to three products, writes about the benefits of each, and ultimately gives their endorsement of one of the three products. Naturally, all three products have affiliate programs, and the trusted source is earning commission by recommending them. (And, in many cases, the one that is the most recommended gives the highest commission!) Review sites, when done well and with integrity, are a win-win for the consumer and affiliate. The consumer gets to get a glimpse into what various programs are like, weighing the pros and cons, and the trusted source earns an income by providing the information. You can see a great review site in action by going to **www.CNET.com.**

Sign Up for a Free Report, Guide, or E-Course

In the marketing world, it is a rule of thumb that it usually takes seven contacts to get someone to convert from a prospect to a customer. This means that one visit to a website usually isn't enough to get the sale. So, in order to keep the customer interested, most marketers offer a free guide or free report. All the prospect has to do is offer up their e-mail address (a real one, of course), and it will be sent immediately through the wonder of digital technology. Once the marketer has the e-mail address, they can then send more and more relevant information about the company, and the products. Contact continues until the prospect tells the marketer they no longer wish to receive e-mail from them.

Pay Per Click Marketing

Pay Per Click (PPC) marketing is where advertisers pay a fee only when their ad is clicked. Unlike the newspaper ads of yore, when you paid a flat rate and your ad was visible for a day or week, etc., the PPC model allows you to set your rate per click, a daily spending limit, and advertise over the Interwebs.

Example: I have an ad that I run for my Mystery Shopping program. I pay $0.25 per click and my daily limit at $50 per day. That means that I should receive no more than 250 views per day. Provided I make at least one sale, I'm earning a profit.

The most popular PPC program is Google's Adwords, but other search engines run them as well. You can see Google's Adwords at work by looking up, well, just about anything on Google. On the left hand side of the page, you'll see the natural search results. On the right-hand side of the page, and the top 2 listings in yellow, you see all of the PPC listings. If you're searching the terms "work at home," many of these links are to affiliate programs.

Websites and blogs can also make money with Google's program, Adwords. There, you'll get paid per click when someone clicks on ads you post on your site. I've made money on both sides of the fence: as an Adsense publisher, and an Adwords advertiser.

Why This Matters

Identifying PPC ads give you more insight into different aspects of Web marketing and how to distinguish opportunities from real jobs. Although you're probably already conditioned to realize that search engine results on the right-hand side seem less "legit" than those on the left, now you know why.

Attending Seminars

Chances are that at some point you've received a post-card, e-mail, or saw an ad online to attend a local seminar in your area about real estate investing, starting your own Internet business, or something along those lines. Granted, seminars are generally an offline technique, but they're pretty powerful and effective, and so it's important that you're aware of the strategies they employ.

The general layout of a seminar is this:

- You get a postcard for very specific dates, times and locations for a seminar usually at a hotel.
- You HAVE to call to register. You'll give them your name, address, phone, and e-mail.
- When you arrive and check in, you may or may not get a free gift. Usually a day-planner, calculator or something along those lines.
- There may or may not be food there. Some are really fancy and have full dinners or luncheons, others just have snacks like cookies or fruit, and some just offer water.
- The presenters will speak, giving good, relevant information about the industry that they're in. This is to show you that they know what they're talking about, to

make you trust them, and to make you feel like you're getting value for your time.

- People who have been involved with the company will get up and speak about the great success they've had with the company. Usually, they've made a lot of money within a small amount of time, and they had a hard obstacle to overcome. A recently divorced single mother, a laid-off worker, or a retiree. (Social proof, anyone?)
- At the end of the seminar, they'll offer various programs so that you too can get involved in the company. They could offer books, classes, or a mentoring program.
- The price of whatever it is that they're offering is usually much higher, but today only, they're offering a really reduced rate! Of course, there are only so many spots available!

After you leave, whether or not you buy, you are on the company's mailing list and will be marketed to after the seminar.

If you do buy, the company may then try to get you to purchase even more products or more in-depth mentoring programs for more money.

I have attended many seminars—at least 40 at this point—and they all follow this formula pretty closely. I have purchased products and training programs from various companies and have had various amounts of success with them. They are fairly low-pressure sales environments, (unlike time shares!), but make no mistake—they will try to sell you something, so be prepared to have marketing techniques manipulate your senses before you walk in the door.

What You Need To Know About Your E-mail

E-mails with Images and HTML

E-mail no longer has to be just boring black words on white backgrounds since many providers allow for HTML (the basic coding language that websites are designed in) and images in messages. Internet marketers love this advancement in technology. Not only does it make their newsletters more pretty and increase brand awareness, but they can now track who is actually opening their e-mails because of the tracking code embedded in the HTML.

It's a very powerful thing—knowing who is opening your mail, the time of day it's opened, and whether or not someone clicks through to buy or sign up for another offer.

However, from the consumer prospective, it can be kind of creepy. And should the e-mail be from a spammer or scammer, they now know that your e-mail address is valid and will be happy to send you many other e-mails with images and HTML pushing their latest thing.

Scammers and spammers also can craft their e-mails to make them look like legitimate businesses. I can't even count how many e-mails I've received from people posing as eBay or Amazon or a random bank with images, logos, and everything! Some will have links that say **www.eBay.com** but, through the joy of HTML, they actually go to **www.ebay.thisisalsoafakewebsite.com**.

I always advise people to have at least two different e-mail addresses: one for friends and family and one for everything else. Disable the images for the second one, and you'll be safer from unwanted marketing ploys. It is usually quite easy to do, just go into the "properties" or "Options" or "help" section of your e-mail inbox and follow the instructions.

When You Mark Something as Spam

E-mail marketing is nearly 100% "permission-based" at this point due to the CAN-SPAM Act of 2003. This means a marketer first has to ask for permission to send messages to a prospect, and the prospect then must "opt-in" to receive those messages. Usually, it happens in a fairly quick process:

- Prospect signs up to receive messages using a form online.
- Prospect is e-mailed a verification link stating it's ok to send messages.
- Prospect clicks on link to verify that he wants messages.
- Prospect is then e-mailed various messages from marketer.

It's a very good system. However, sometimes prospects don't remember that they signed up for a particular online newsletter, or just get tired of receiving messages or for whatever reason decide to label a particular piece of e-mail SPAM.

When that happens, the marketer is "dinged" for sending spam. If you get a certain percentage of "dings" (I think it's about 1-5%, but it varies with each company), the marketer's e-mail distributor may shut them down. Using the 5% example, that means it takes only 5 people out of 100 to mark a message as spam before a marketer is then re-evaluated by their e-mail distributor and perhaps shut down. Of course, it would take a history of consistent complaints to warrant such measures, but just keep these things in mind before you jump so quickly to mark something as spam. Your actions can really hurt those of us who are trying to abide by the Internet marketing rules of good conduct.

On the converse side, not marking legitimate spam as spam can have adverse effects as well. When you label e-mails that come to your inbox as spam, you are training spam guard programs on how to recognize new patterns of deceit. This is especially helpful to protect people against scammers.

The bottom line is this: if something is really and truly spam, mark it! It helps your fellow Internet citizens figure out the scammers among us. If something isn't legitimately spam, DON'T mark it just because you don't remember signing up for a newsletter, or you don't like the content or whatever. It will help legitimate marketers be able to get their message out.

You can learn more about spam, known IP addresses that engage in heavy spamming, and what we're trying to do about it by visiting **www.spamhaus.org**: A non-profit agency dedicated to tracking spammers.

Free E-mail Accounts

I have several free email accounts. Yahoo is my provider of choice, but Gmail, Hotmail, and Juno all provide really great services as well for personal matters. When it comes to business, you better believe that I have professional e-mail addresses hosted through my domains.

When you are looking for fun random and work-from-home jobs online, be wary job offers from a free e-mail account, as well as any subdomains that may be disguised in a fake website (**bob@yahoo.fictionalwebsite.com**) and be *especially* aware of Gmail accounts!

Gmail created an extra layer of protection for its users, so when you try to trace a Gmail e-mail (we discussed the specifics in a previous chapter), it will ALWAYS go back to the Gmail server. So, instead of being able to track down a would-be scammer, they are doubly protected when using a Gmail account.

I am NOT saying that everyone who uses a Gmail account is a spammer. I have a Gmail account, as does my sister. However, if you receive e-mails about work from home jobs from a Gmail account the sender is much more likely to be a spammer than not, simply because it's much harder to get caught.

(The End of the) Free Reign of Internet Marketing

In the offline world, there are strict regulations for marketers. You see commercials on TV that boast big claims, but in teeny tiny print those dubious words, "results not typical" or "elapsed time, 45 minutes." Or you see in a magazine a full-page article spouting off the amazingness of some new wonder drug, but right at the top, in bold letters it says ADVERTISEMENT.

Offline marketing has had established rules and regulations for years. However, it wasn't until December 1, 2009 that the new regulations for bloggers and Internet marketers went into place. These regulations give requirements for testimonials, endorsements, and reasonable expectation of results from a product or service being advertised. The following (shortened) links will give you direct information from the FTC regarding these rules:

FTC document, "Dot Com Disclosures": **http://bit.ly/rKUJIh**
FTC endorsement guide: **http://1.usa.gov/w1FYI**

CAN-SPAM Laws

In 2003, Congress enacted a bill that set up regulations for how businesses are able to contact customers and prospects through e-mail. I will defer to the Federal Trade Commission's website (**www.ftc.gov/bcp/edu/pubs/business/ecommerce/bus61.shtm)** that fully explains the rules and regulations, but here is a summary of the guidelines:

Don't use false or misleading e-mail headers. Unless your e-mail is actually about Britney Spears, you can't use her name to get a reader's attention. The same applies to using phrases such as "Your account has been suspended."

Identify the message as an ad. If you are trying to sell something, you must state somewhere in the e-mail that it is an advertisement. Just like in magazines, where there are full-page ads that look like articles, there is also a statement either at the top or bottom of the ad stating ADVERTISEMENT.

Tell recipients where you're located. You must provide a current street mailing address.

Tell recipients how to opt out of receiving future e-mail from you. You must provide information on how a recipient can stop receiving e-mail from you, either by contacting you directly or through an opt-out link that you provide.

Honor opt-out requests promptly. You must remove people from your mailing list at their request, within a certain time frame, i.e., you can't take two months to remove someone from your list.

Monitor what others are doing on your behalf. If you hire a person or company to take care of your e-mail marketing, you must make sure that they adhere to the CAN-SPAM laws. Otherwise, you are both liable for any violations.

Chapter 6
Common Job-Related Scams

When you're looking at work at home jobs and opportunities out in the real world, I really want you to think of things from an employer's point of view. Why would they hire someone to do this work? What benefit are they getting to have someone work from home? If they don't interview you, or if it's only an e-mail interview, why? If they don't check for references, why? When you put yourself in their place, it's easy to see how these common scams are simply not legit.

Chain Letters/Pyramid Schemes

The most well-known defrauder in history, Charles Ponzi, would promise great returns on investments that didn't exist. He paid current investors with new investor money, completing the cycle. Of course, at some point it had to fail, since there are a finite number of people in the world, but Ponzi was wildly successful until he got caught in 1910. Although he never achieved his monetary goals, Charles Ponzi remains forever in history, as many examples of this scam are simply labeled "Ponzi Schemes."

Chain letters are less prevalent through the mail now but can still be found online. You receive a notice with a list of names and instructions to send $5 to the person at the top of the list. You then remove their name, put yours on the bottom, and then send the notice to 10 other people to do the same. In theory, once your name gets to the top of the list, you'll get lots of money. There are variations of this: instead of sending a set dollar amount to the person at the top, you may be requested to send money to each individual listed. Whatever it entails, just know that it doesn't work and it's illegal!

Envelope Stuffing

This probably is the granddaddy of all scams. And I'll admit it, when I was at college, I sent away $19.95 so that I could become a millionaire stuffing envelopes at home. I know it's shocking, but it didn't work out the way I thought.

Envelope stuffing is just a twist on the chain-letter scam. The information that I received told me that all I had to do was take out an ad, just like the one that I responded to, and collect money sending the recipients the same notice I got. That's it. How simple! Of course, they neglected to mention that this is against the law.

Since there is no legitimate way of earning income, just asking people to send you money and do the same thing you're doing, it's just a big old scam. Now, there are other companies, as I have learned through the years, who WILL actually pay you to stuff envelopes. What they neglect to mention is that this is unsolicited mail, usually containing some form of porn. Most people aren't comfortable doing that, so the company neglects to mention what the industry is actually about, they'll take your money, and run.

Let's be logical here. Why would *anyone* pay *anyone* $1 to $4 per envelope just to stuff it? What guarantee do they have that you're actually doing the work? If I was a business owner paying someone that much to do something *so* trivial, I would want to be sure that the work was getting done!

Assembling Products from Home

I know you've seen the ads. Somewhere in the depths of the "Classified" section, there it is, calling out to you, "Assemble Products at home. No experience necessary. Make $200–$2000 a week!" You get giddy. By all accounts you're competent, independent, and reliable. You need this job. You can do this job. The only problem is that these people LIE.

The whole concept of this scam is that you'll buy a package from them, ranging from $20–$100. You have to pay a fee because the company needs to be "covered" in case the materials get lost or damaged. They also want to make sure that you'll actually do the work, after all, it cost them money, and they need to be able to recoup their costs. It's logical; it makes sense. The company will even tell you that after you return the products you'll receive not only your payment, but the initial fee you put forth, plus shipping and handling, since you were so reliable. But no matter what sense you were given, you begin to think it's a good deal.

Believe me, it doesn't matter what it is that you're assembling, it could be CD cases, jewelry, toys, whatever—the end result is always the same.

You ship the package back, waiting for their "approval." After all, they need to make sure that your work is up to their "quality standards." They take their own sweet time getting back to you. When you contact them to find out where your check is, they tell you, "Oh, it wasn't up to our specifications."

Don't believe for one second that they threw away your products. If you did a decent job, they will be sold. And wasn't that nice of you? Not only did you work for free, you actually paid the assembly company to work for them.

Ad Placement/Processing E-mails/Data Entry/Virtual Assistant

This "job" comes in many forms, but what it boils down to is an electronic version of the old envelope stuffing scam.

Essentially, the job offer tells you that the company is just so busy that they simply can't process their own e-mails. They need help running ads and responding to inquiries. There is a fee, generally somewhat minimal, for training or processing your information, or a membership fee or whatever. Once it's received, you are given instructions on how you can run your very own ad and have people send you money. Nice, huh?

Just so you know, virtual assistants do actually exist. If you find a company advertising for one, check it out thoroughly before applying. The company shouldn't charge you any fees just for the joy and privilege of working for them. Remember, the company is supposed to be paying you!

Job Placement Scams

This scam is the reason why most legitimate job-placement companies run statements at the bottom of their ad stating, "Never a fee to applicants!"

It's simple, really—companies will claim that they have work available in certain fields, and they'll place prospective employees for a fee. The fee is collected, and no job is ever given. The company gets away with it because maybe the potential position was filled by someone else, or the employer decided to withdraw, or the economy is just tough right now. The big annoyance is when there is a recurring monthly charge to your credit card, instead of a one-time fee, and you have to continually fight to get it refunded.

Medical Billing/Transcription

Many people get started in medical billing because they already had their foot in the door as a current or former health care worker. They already knew the industry, knew some contacts in the field, and simply offered to reduce the billing costs of a few clinics. If you want to get into medical transcription, you'll need to know medical terminology, anatomy, insurance coding (each procedure performed has a certain code), and knowledge of how to complete various forms. You can get training for this field either through community colleges, or online courses. (Check out Part III)

The scams around medical billing deal with the companies who promise to give you everything you need to start your own business. For $400–$10,000 (depending on the ad), they'll give you the software, supplies, training and contacts to get you started. If the materials actually do arrive, they're either not used in the industry, or well below sufficient for what's needed, or just plain defective. The list of doctors that use at home billing agents is usually too old to be useful, and you're out of a lot of money.

Remember, medical billing is a work-at-home *opportunity*. You'll still need to go out and find your clients. You'll need to give great customer service. There may be some clinics and organizations that post ads for medical billing from home, but they're rare, so be sure to check out any ad that you do see to the fullest extent.

Payment Processing/Payroll Clerk/Check Cashing

You may receive an e-mail or see an ad online from a company that needs someone in your area to process checks or rebates or act as a payroll clerk. Usually the company that is hiring you is overseas, and it says it needs a representative in the U.S. or Canada to handle payments since it can't. Regardless of where the company is located, it's going to get you, so don't assume that just because it is in the U.S. that it's legit.

There are a couple of different versions on how you'll be taken or how you'll be assisting in the scamming of others. Keep in mind that these are pretty sophisticated scams, so you may only be one part of the larger puzzle:

1) As a payment processing clerk, you may be asked to set up a bank account at a specific bank to receive direct deposits or to handle expenses. The company who "hired" you will put money in the bank account, and then you're supposed to wire that money through Western Union to other employees, vendors, or companies. In reality, you're just wiring it to the scammers. When a company requires you to have a specific bank for your direct deposit, keep in mind that the scammers may have hacked into that bank and electronically transferred money into your account. Once the bank realizes what has happened, YOU will be liable to repay those funds. If you're required to use a specific bank, contact that bank and let it know that you suspect it may have been hacked.
2) You may be asked to act as a payroll clerk and process checks at home. You'll be required to purchase checks and a software system, and the company will mail you the names, bank information, and the amount of money to send to employees. Be aware of the amounts of money on these checks, usually $500 and up. This is because the scammer is using you to create these fake checks, and the recipient will be required to wire a portion of that check back to the scammer. You, of course, are unaware of all of this. All you know is that you have to mail checks. They look real, but they're not.

3) You may be asked to be a money transfer agent. You'll be required to pick up money at a Western Union and then wire it somewhere else. In this case, you're just a mule—you take the money that's wired from someone else who received a fake check, and you'll be wiring it to the scammers.

Hopefully, you can see a theme here: Western Union. This is because money through Western Union is really hard to get back. The scammers would never send you checks or use credit card information, because it's too easy to track. If ever you come across a situation where Western Union (or any other type of money-transfer company) is involved: RUN.

Get Paid To Try

"Get Paid to Try" is a blanket term I use in describing the offers that claim to pay you to try out their services or offers. While you can make some money with them, many are set up to be confusing and deceptive, and you really have to be organized in order to make more than you spend. In my personal opinion, it's too complicated for the amount of money you'd make. But, anyone can do it, so here's what you need to know:

There are sites online where you can sign up to try out offers (like through Netflix, or FreeCreditReport), and they'll pay you a small fee. In some cases, you may have to pay shipping and handling, but you'll net more than you spend. For example, the company will pay you $8 to try something out, but shipping and handling is $4.95, so you net $3.05. (Woo-hoo! Don't spend it all in one place!)

The trial period may be four days, two weeks, or a month, and you may have to give your credit card information because if you don't cancel before the trial period is over, it will charge you a monthly fee to continue using the product. The company is banking on the fact that you'll either really like the product so you'll stay with it or forget that you need to cancel your trial membership so it will get more money that way.

In some cases, it's really hard to cancel your membership, and in others the system may have errors so you're not properly credited for the services you try out. In most cases, once you get on these e-mail lists, you'll be bombarded with more and more offers.

I once signed on for something like this through my credit card company, where I had to just try "Great Rewards" for 30 days for free, and they would send me a $10 check. If I didn't cancel, I would be billed $39 or so a month right to my credit card.

Luckily, it was easy to cancel the trial membership, so no worries there, but the $10 check that I received was just another trial offer for 30 days. If I cashed the check, I agreed to be enrolled in the program for 30 days, and if I didn't cancel my membership I would be bill for $39 monthly. What a ridiculous cycle. I did think about continuing on it (they actually sent me quite a few of these offers), but I know myself (and the telemarketing industry) and I know at some point, I would be billed for $39 and just get really annoyed at the whole thing. I just don't think it's worth it.

While I don't recommend them, there are some legitimate "get paid to try" companies in Part II.

Surveys

If you've ever done any kind of market research, you know the legitimacy of focus groups, mystery shopping, and exit interviews. More than once I'd gather, you've been approached in the mall by someone who is desperate for your opinion on their latest soap or movie or food.

It's a completely legitimate practice: finding out a consumers opinion so that you can decide how best to position your company for optimum profits. This is real. People do get paid for it. Some people make really good money at it; others get swindled into the dungeons of Internet surveying.

This industry is a little bit tricky because some companies are moving their market research online. There are legitimate opportunities out there, but a little harder to find. (Check out Part II for more information.) Before we go any further, I must state that you should never have to pay anyone to do market research. If they're asking for money, it's something you don't need. Keep in mind, though, that some Internet research companies don't require payment, but they'll still scam you.

What I have found with the majority of "Get Paid for Your Opinion" companies is that they'll set your minimum payment at about $100. This makes sense, as most surveys only have maybe a $0.50–$5 payment for them, and a company doesn't want to have to send out checks for such a minimal amount. They'll state this when you first sign up, and start sending you TONS of surveys. You start filling them out left and right, thinking, "Oh my gosh, this is so EASY! I've found the Holy Grail!" All of a sudden, you notice that your payment is up to $80! In just a few days! But then the surveys stop coming.

You never hear from the company again. Even after you contact them, update your contact information, do whatever you have to do—you'll never get that money. You'll never get the chance to reach the $100 minimum payment amount because the company has taken you off their list.

Credit Check Required

It's becoming common for companies to require credit checks and/or background checks of potential employees. Especially if you are applying for a work-at-home position where you'll be taking orders over the phone and handling customer's credit cards or other sensitive information.

If a company provides you a specific link for you to click on to get your credit report, it may be a scam. They may have created the site and rigged it to steal your info, or they may just be directing you to a site where they earn commission off of the credit report. You can get your own credit report by contacting the three major credit bureaus: Experian, TransUnion, and Equifax.

Some scammers have caught on that we don't want to click on the links they provide, so they'll take a different approach. They may ask you to get your own credit report, black out your social security number and then send them the info. Don't do this. Even with your social security number off your report, the scammer will learn about every single bank account you've ever had (and sometimes the account number), every single credit card you ever had, as well as it's balance and credit limit, and every single address you ever lived at. That's just way too much personal information for a potential employer to have.

Again, it's not necessarily a scam if a company asks for your credit report, but make sure you have met with your employers, done your due diligence on the company, and have a firm job-offer in place before consenting.

Mystery Shopping

Mystery shopping is where regular people are hired to pretend like they're customers and give objective evaluations on products and services they receive. It is a real way to make extra money. I should know considering I've worked for over 150 companies and have been shopping since 1999!

One thing to keep in mind is that mystery shopping companies do not advertise for jobs on Yahoo, CareerBuilder, Craigslist, or any other resume job-type site. There are specific websites where mystery shopping companies post their assignments, and mystery shopping assignments DON'T involve wiring money!!! Mystery shopping companies do not pay by cashier's check (usually it's a regular check, PayPal, or direct deposit), and you are not required to have any certification to be a shopper.

The main mystery shopping scam involves you shopping a Western Union or other money transfer business. As you learned earlier with the payroll processing scam, you need to avoid anything to do with Western Union like the plague. The scam is quite simple: you'll be asked to mystery shop a Western Union. They'll send you a check that's looks so real, the teller won't suspect it's a fake. The amount will be enough to cover your "mystery shop" fee and whatever amount they need sent through Western Union. For example, they may give you a $1,500 check, say that $500 is your fee, and you need to wire $1,000 through Western Union. Since the check is not good to begin with, you're actually wiring your own $1,000 to the scammer.

Most mystery shops pay $10–$50 each, not $500. If you see this scam, run. If you want more info on mystery shopping and how to get started, visit my website: **www.QueenoftheRandomJob.com**

Chapter 7
Payment Scams

While these scams have nothing to do with employment, I felt the need to include them as they're extremely common. Nearly every time I run an ad, I'm bombarded with scammers trying to take advantage of me. They all have common threads that deal with using money orders and/or being from overseas.

Payment scams come in many forms:

- Someone who wants to buy a large-ticket item and have it shipped.
- A long-distance apartment renter or roommate.
- A potential lover or soul mate.
- A long-lost relative who left you an inheritance.

For Sale Ads

When my parents moved, they asked me to help them sell a lot of their big-ticket items online. One such item was an obnoxiously huge TV set. I honestly don't remember the dimensions, but it had to be at least four feet long because I remember it barely fitting into the closet that ran along the back wall of the room.

We had it advertised on Craigslist for somewhere around $1000. The very first response I got was from a guy in Ireland who wanted to purchase the TV for his daughter as a graduation present. Since he was in Ireland, he understood that I couldn't take a check and would be more than happy to send me a cashier's check to cover shipping as well as the price of the item.

I refer to this scam as the "Overpayment" scam. The offender will send a cashier's check in an amount greater than requested, and the seller will return the overpaid amount, along with the item.

Luckily, my momma didn't raise no fool, and I simply e-mailed the guy back and let him know that the TV weighed over 400 pounds and he was insane to think I would even consider shipping it to Ireland. Of course, this happened several years ago, and now when I get these e-mails, I just ignore them, since I don't really want these scammers to have access to my real e-mail account anyway.

When I told my Mom the story, she asked me how I knew that it was a scam. I told her that it simply didn't make sense. Why would someone ship a large-screen TV overseas? And after doing some research, I figured out how the scam worked.

By the way, this applies to all items for sale, big or small, cheap or expensive. If someone offers to send you a cashier's check or money order, beware! Stick to PayPal if you can't take cash in person.

For Rent Ads

When I was helping a friend rent his apartment, I had an experience much like my Irish adventure in TV-land. It seemed that many people who answered my ad were from out of town (or overseas) and were more than happy to send me a money order to cover first and last month's rent as well as another other necessary deposits. Of course, they were just trying to overpay me, so I would return the excess funds to them.

At this point, I just shake my head and wonder if they really think we're that stupid? Especially since now everyone can take PayPal for payment processing!

When you're looking as a renter at a new home be sure to do your research before handing over any money. I have heard countless stories about individuals who moved into a place that had been vacant, thinking they were dealing with the owner. In fact, it was just a scam artist who collected the rent and then took off. As time goes on, the people who moved into the space are either evicted by the true owners, or forced to move because the home goes into foreclosure.

If you're looking for a new place to live, make sure you are dealing with the true owners of the home and know that it is on solid financial footing before moving in.

Dating Ads

I am extremely lucky that I have never encountered someone trying to use me romantically to get to my massive wads of cash. (Of course, it might be because I don't have massive wads of cash, but, whatever.)

I have only heard about these cons through various news reports, and can only imagine the heartache of being deceived by someone you love. Stupidity, however, comes into play if you allow yourself to develop feelings through e-mail and phone communication only. So many of these victims allow themselves to "fall in love" and turn over savings, credit card information, or resources to help their betrothed get into the country or just their local area.

To be clear, I have absolutely nothing against online dating. In this day and age it is a perfectly reasonable method for people to meet, but use some caution before you bare your soul and lose your wallet!

Door-to-Door Cons

These cons are more than annoying because they happen right at your doorstep! People have posed as magazine salesmen, utility operators, collection agencies, exterminators, census workers, and more just to get access to the inside of your home. They could be scoping it out for a future robbery, or inflict intimidation to get you to pay money up front for some work that they absolutely have to do on the house. These types of people tend to prefer to prey on the elderly since it is easier for them to get confused. No matter who comes to your door, verify everything and use common sense. Call a neighbor for help if you need to, but make sure you don't get caught up in one of these scams!

Lottery Scams

Congratulations! You may already be a winner! Aren't you excited? Have you decided how to spend your winnings yet? Not so fast there, Rockefeller. These are plain and simple scams. Many of which, unfortunately, prey on the elderly.

People are contacted every day through e-mail, mail, and over the telephone with notifications that they have won money. Keep in mind that lotteries are regulated, and you cannot win a lottery unless you enter one. When you enter you usually pay for a ticket, and receive a numbered receipt. Sweepstakes, however, are promotional events. No matter what, there needs to be some sort of participation on YOUR END in order to win a prize.

What happens in these scams is that someone is notified they won, and then are told that they need to pay a processing fee in order to get the funds. Since the amount won is usually several hundred thousand dollars or more, the winner doesn't mind forking over $10,000–$20,000 to get the rest. Of course, there is no prize. The winner becomes a big loser when they turn over the money and see that they get nothing in return.

Long-Lost Relatives

Let's just make one thing really, really clear, okay? You do not now nor have you ever had an uncle/cousin/sister-in-law or other relative, distant relative, or friend of a distant relative that was once an important official/king/queen/random person who had a lot of money/major inheritance/or discovered a treasure in a far-away country/kingdom/deserted island/sunken boat that wants to give you a portion of the spoils if only you could front the transaction cost.

Not to diminish your family tree in any way, but the chances of this are just not that great.

This is just a phishing ploy, trying to get that one sucker out of a million who will gladly pay $10,000 for the chance of making millions.

You may be the princess of your own little world, but on here on earth, you'll just lose a lot of money in this scam.

Chapter 8
How to Identify Scams: SCRAM™

After being an independent contractor for more than a decade, I've developed a sort of second sense when it comes to identifying scams. It's not hard for me to gloss over a posting, e-mail, or "opportunity" to decipher what is real and worth my time. I get requests all the time to help others do the same, and it really comes down to simple common sense, easily determined by my SCRAM™ formula.

S Scrutinize the source
C Check for affiliate links and fees
R Research the heck out of every little bit of information they give you
A Ask for more info
M Mouse over images and links to see where they really go!

Let's look at these in-depth before we move onto real-life examples.

S = Scrutinize the Source

I mentioned before that my father worked as a newspaper editor for 40 years before retiring. He instilled in me a heavy dose of skepticism when it comes to believing things blindly. Your first role, when looking at a job ad is to completely and un-objectively scrutinize the source. This means, you need to consider where you got the information about the job or opportunity from, the motives they have for you to view it, and the content inside the ad.

- Papers like the *Pennysaver, U.S. Weekly, The Globe,* and other entertainment magazines are full of scams and MLM-type opportunities.

- Local newspapers have more legitimate offerings, but also are looking for people to start their own businesses in direct sales.
- Google's paid search results (at the very top and on the right-hand side) are paid ads from people usually trying to sell something or develop their marketing lists.
- Google's natural search results (on the left-hand side) are compiled by a complex algorithm by people much smarter than you and I, and have a little more legitimacy.
- Receiving a job offer in your e-mail (spam or not) can be a sign of a phishing attempt. "Phishing" is when a scammer sends out thousands of e-mails (or "lures") to potential victims in hopes that just one will "take the bait."
- Receiving a job offer as a response to your posted resume can also be a sign of a phishing attempt.
- A friend told you about them. While we love our friends and family, they're as clueless as we are in regards to identifying scams. How many times have you been sent an e-mail stating that Bill Gates wants to share his fortune? Exactly. While everyone likes to help you during your job search, take their recommendations with a grain of salt.
- On TV or radio: as an ad or infomercial. Again, from a company usually trying to sell something or boost its marketing list.
- On TV or radio: as an interview. Companies get on TV for publicity, not because they are looking to hire.
- Craigslist and other online job boards may be free to post on, (depending on your city) so they can be teeming with scams. (I talk about how Craigslist's job posts are laid out in Part III.)
- Did they contact you or did you contact them? Scammers use Yahoo, Monster, and other resume posting services to find people who are looking for jobs. **www.LinkedIn.com** is a little more reputable as people have to belong to a company or have networks of people you can contact as well, but don't trust it completely. Within moments of setting up my LinkedIn account, I had a job offer from an overseas company.
- What time of day did they post or contact you? If it's not normal business hours wherever you are (or a little on either side), then they might be overseas. Most Job ads on Craigslist posted between 10 p.m. and 5 a.m. get flagged down pretty quickly.

- How many spelling or grammatical errors are there? How formal is the language of the post or e-mail? It's quite common for those abroad to use more formal language than we're used to. If you see British spelling, or notice phrases like, "I humbly request your answer, and trust that you are most suited for our company" it's a near guarantee that they're not a real company.

C = Check for Affiliate Links, Fees, and Surveys

This next step is to make sure that you understand if the offer is a job or an opportunity. If there is a survey that you need to fill out in order to be considered for the job, fill it out with fake information first. Sometimes, scammers will get your contact information first through a survey, and then send you a link to an affiliate program, or something to purchase once everything went through. And then, they have your e-mail address to market to!

That's not to say that every company who uses a survey is a scammer. I've found them to be extremely effective in weeding out people who don't have the right skill set. However, others use them just to get your contact information, and then send you an automatic e-mail with links to buy their stuff. It's pretty sneaky and frankly, deplorable.

Refer to Chapter 4 for information on how to check and research affiliate links.

R = Research the Heck Out of Every Detail!

There are so many resources available to you to determine whether a company is real or not, just based on the information they give you. Here are some things you can do.

Check the company's e-mail. If it's "**staples@gmail.com**" it's not really from the corporate "Staples" company. No corporation would be caught dead with a free e-mail account. If it's from something like "**info@ebay.thisisafakewebsite.com**", remember that the last portion of the e-mail address is really the domain name. The "eBay" portion is just a subdomain, whereas the "thisisafakewebsite.com" is the actual domain. And don't forget, Gmail is the scammer's e-mail address of choice!

Check out the company's website. Really look through it and actually call the phone number that's listed to make sure it's real. You can also research the number at **www.whocallsme.com** to see what other people have to say about the number. Go to **www.whois.com** or **www.dnstools.com** to look up the domain and see how long it's been active.

What do other people have to say about it? Visit **www.RipoffReport.com** or **www.BadBusinessBureau.com** to see if it's listed.

Google the heck out of every piece of information the website gives: its phone and fax numbers, its address, its website, the contact person's name and city (are they on it says it works with. It really just takes five minutes to learn about this potential employer. Do your research!

Look up its IP address in **www.ARIN.net** to see if it's really located where it says it is. It's not always going to give you exact information, but if the company is really overseas, and it's telling you it's in Georgia, you'll be able to know it's lying. You can also look up companies and IP addresses at **www.SpamHaus.org** to see if they're known spammers. (Refer to Chapter 5 on how to track IP and e-mail addresses.)

Does the business have anything to do with money orders? Either sending or receiving? If so, STAY AWAY!

Are they offering obscenely good rates for entry-level work? If it's a data-entry position paying $25 per hr and $12/hr is typical for your area, it's probably a scam.

A = Ask for More Information

If the company doesn't tell you enough in its ad, contact them politely with a different name and e-mail address to get more information. This is especially effective with job boards, when companies may not list their contact information. That way when they e-mail you back, you can research their e-mail and IP address to know if they are indeed a real company or a waste of time. Once you make that initial contact, you can then contact them again with your real information, confident that you'll be safe from scammers.

Keep in mind that since so many people are applying for jobs now, you may not actually hear back from the company. Sometimes I feel like if I don't hear from a company, they may actually be legitimate, because scammers will take any opportunity to keep you interested!

M = Mouse Over Images and Links

When you mouse over an image or a link, you'll see the destination in the bottom of the browser. If the company is proclaiming to be PayPal, but its links go to **http://www.PayPa1.com,** then you know you're dealing with a scammer. Scammers are clever! Instead of using an "l" they might just use a capital "i" or a number "1" to see if it can get by your quick glance, so really look hard at those links. By the way, the domain **www.Paypa1.com** is currently owned by PayPal. I don't believe that has always been the case, however. There are many scammers who try to cash in on brand confusion by registering similar domain names of well-known companies, and PayPal (as well as other banking institutions) is a large target.

While you're mousing around, don't forget to look for affiliate links or check to see if the links are cloaked with **www.tinyurl.com** or **www.bit.ly**. Affiliate programs aren't necessarily scams, but they'll just waste your time if you're looking for an actual job.

Example:

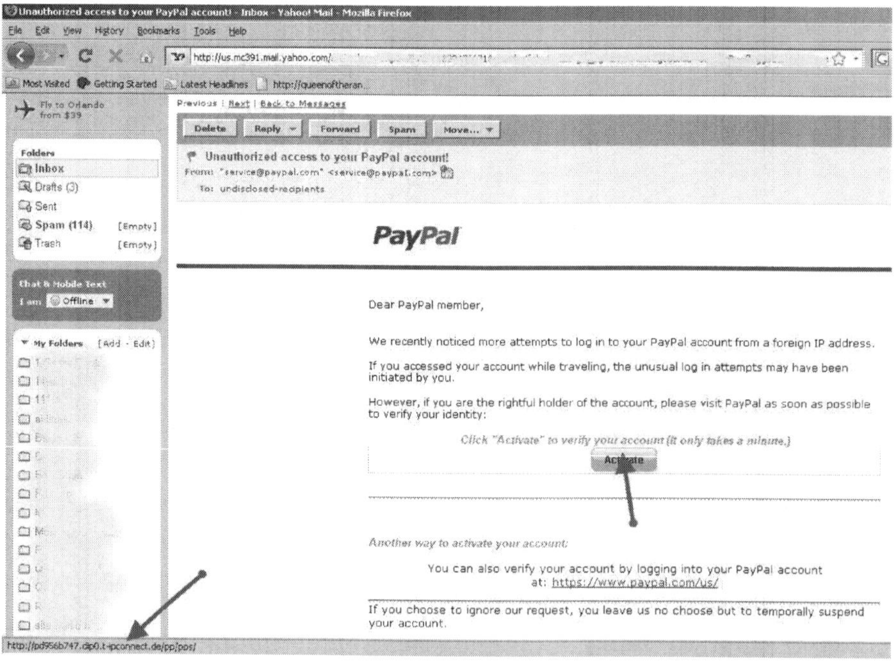

This email looks like it is coming from Paypal because of the images used. However, when mousing over the "Activate" button (which is both an image and a link), you'll see the destination of that link in the lower left corner. In this case it's: **http://pd956b747.dip0.t-ipconnect.de/pp/pps/** "pd956b747" is a subdomain "dip0" is a subdomain "t-ipconnect" is the domain ".de" is the extension, which belongs to Germany, just like ".us" belongs to the United States. If it really was from Paypal, the link would go to Paypal, and not a random site in Germany!

When you follow these simple SCRAM™ steps, you'll be well on your way to figuring out whether companies are really looking for an employee, are trying to sell you on an opportunity, or just want to scam you. Once you get in the habit of using these tools, it will become second nature and you'll never have to ask yourself again, "Is this real or a scam?"

Chapter 9
Real-Life Encounters of the Scamming Kind

To find real-life examples of common scams, I only had to look as far as my own email. Throughout the next few pages, you'll see various screen-shots of scammers I found (quite easily, unfortunately) with notes on how I was able to identify them as a scam. (Side note: I have blurred out personal information for privacy reasons, you don't need to adjust your eyes!)

Live and learn!

EXAMPLE #1: Distant Relative Left Me Money

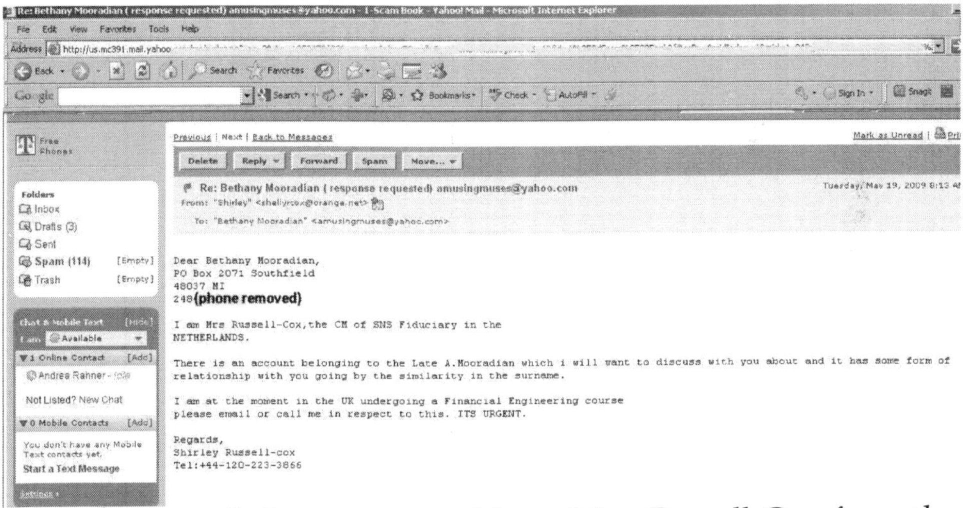
Re: Bethany Mooradian (response requested) amusingmuses@yahoo.com
From: "Shirley" <shellyrcox@orange.net>
To: "Bethany Mooradian" <amusingmuses@yahoo.com>
Tuesday, May 19, 2009 8:13 AM

Dear Bethany Mooradian,
PO Box 2071 Southfield
48037 MI
248{phone removed}

I am Mrs Russell-Cox,the CM of SNS Fiduciary in the NETHERLANDS.

There is an account belonging to the Late A.Mooradian which i will want to discuss with you about and it has some form of relationship with you going by the similarity in the surname.

I am at the moment in the UK undergoing a Financial Engineering course please email or call me in respect to this. ITS URGENT.

Regards,
Shirley Russell-cox
Tel:+44-120-223-3866

In this e-mail, I am contacted by a Mrs. Russell-Cox from the Netherlands that has an issue with an account belonging to a distant relative of mine.

What Made It Almost Feel Real

- My full name was listed, which was not tied to this particular e-mail address.
- A real, full, former address was listed.
- A real, full, former phone number was listed.

How I Knew It Was a Scam

- My last name is as common as "Smith," as far as Armenian surnames are concerned.
- The address and phone number listed was what I used to register domain names, so anyone could have looked it up and gotten the information.
- Come on! A distant relative in the Netherlands? I'm not that naïve!

EXAMPLE #2: Bank of America Wants My Feedback

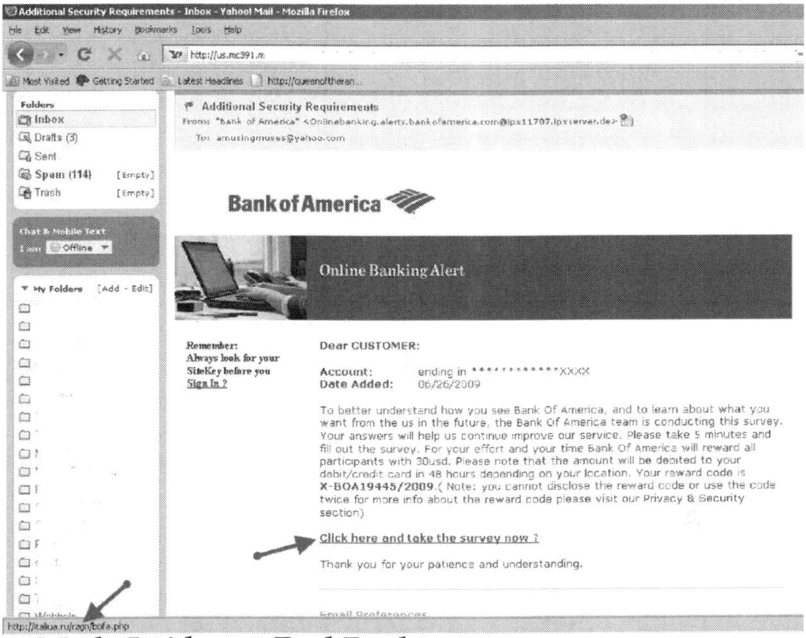

What Made It Almost Feel Real

- The images are Bank of America's real logos, making it look professional and legitimate.

How I Knew It Was a Scam

- When you look closely at the email address, you see it's from **Onlinebanking.alerts.bankofamerica.com@ipx11707.ipxserver.de,** probably the most convoluted e-mail I have ever seen. The .de domain is from Germany, so I knew it wasn't legit.
- When I moused over the "click here and take the survey now" link, it showed the true address as **http://italiua.ru/rzgn/bofa.php** (noted by the arrows). The domain ending in .ru is for Russia, just like .us is for the United States. As far as I know, "Bank of AMERICA" does not have any offices in Russia.
- The most obvious reason: I don't have a Bank of America account!

EXAMPLE #3: An Ad on Craigslist Has the Ideal Work-From-Home Job!

In this post on Craigslist, Costa Coffee with an address in London, England is looking for someone to act as their United States representative. The job entails receiving Money Orders and Cashier's checks, which would be cashed into an account, and then Costa Coffee would then be wired the funds, less payment to the employee.

Part Time Job (seattle-tacoma) Wednesday, May 13, 2009 9:39 PM
From: "amusingmuses@yahoo.com" <amusingmuses@yahoo.com>
To: amusingmuses@yahoo.com

amusingmuses@yahoo.com has forwarded you this craigslist.org posting.
Please see below for more information

Part Time Job

Reply to:
Date: 2009-05-13, 9:17PM
Costa Coffee,
Exporters of Cocoa.
20 Holloway Road
London
N8 8DB.
Phone: +447031978873
Dear Sir/Madam,
We are recruiting individuals to work for the Company as a representative/Book Keeper in the United States We have Customers we Supply Weekly around the world. Our Customers make payments for our Supplies every Week in form of Money Orders, Bankers Draft and Cashier's Checks, Checks which are not Readily Cashable Outside the United States and the country of issuance.
So we need Someone in the States and and the above listed Countries to work as our representative and Assist us in processing the payments from Our Customers and COSTA COFFEE PLC. is offering 10% of the payment received which will be your percentage/pay on Payment processed.
After establishing close co-operation you'll be able to operate with larger orders and you'll be able to earn more Our payments will be issued out in your name and you get them cashed in your bank deduct your weekly salary and forward the balance to the company via Western Union money transfer or Money gram money transfer.
This job takes only 3-7 hours per week
NB: If you are interested, please fill up the form below and get back to me as soon as possible. Endeavour to send your reply through my e-mail address (info.costaemployment2@gmail.com)
APPLICATION FORM
FIRST NAME..........................
LASTNAME...............
ADDRESS.......
CITY...
STATE.......................................
ZIP CODE.......................................
COUNTRY....................................
PHONE NUMBER (S) ....
GENDER................................ MARITAL
STATUS ....
AGE..
NATIONALITY...............................

Regards,
Costa Coffee
Please email me back at (info.costaemployment2@gmail.com) Costa Coffee, Exporters of Quality Cofee.
Costa Coffee

Thank you.

- Location: seattle-tacoma
- Compensation: 10%
- This is a part-time job.
- OK for recruiters to contact this job poster.
- Please, no phone calls about this job!
- Please do not contact job poster about other services, products or commercial interests

Original URL: http://seattle.craigslist.org/see/csr/1169975730.html

---

this craigslist posting was forwarded to you by someone using our email-a-friend feature - if you want to prevent these, please go to:
http://www.craigslist.org/cgi-bin/te/11WYul2c112ZzV2cnIHGv9GavNmLAAQbR

What Made It Almost Feel Real

- They give a lot of information in the advertisement.
- There is a real Costa Coffee in London (found out after I looked them up), and they actually distribute to Starbucks!

How I Knew It Was a Scam

- The company is located overseas.
- The job deals with cashier's checks and money orders. (Apparently their customers have never heard of a credit card.)
- The e-mail address to contact for further information is a Gmail account.
- On their list of questions to answer, they ask for marital status and nationality. It is illegal to ask anyone those questions on a job application in the U.S. since it violates Federal Equal Employment Opportunity laws.
- Even though the company really does exist, I have a sneaky feeling that scammers are just using real companies to thwart savvy Web goers while they research these ads. Someone might be willing to overlook the Gmail e-mail address if they feel that the company actually exists.

EXAMPLE #4: PayPal Wants to Protect My Account

I received a notice from PayPal telling me that there have been too many logon attempts from a foreign IP address. They want me to update my account as soon as possible (see PayPal Image #1).

What Made It Almost Feel Real

- The images are really PayPal's logos (see PayPal Image #2).
- When I mouse over the "update preferences" link, the link actually goes to the PayPal site (see PayPal Image #1).

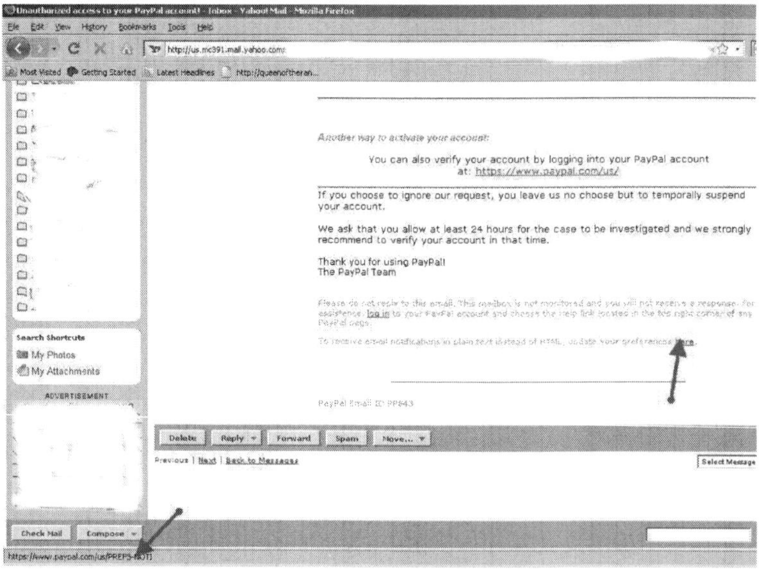

PayPal Image #1

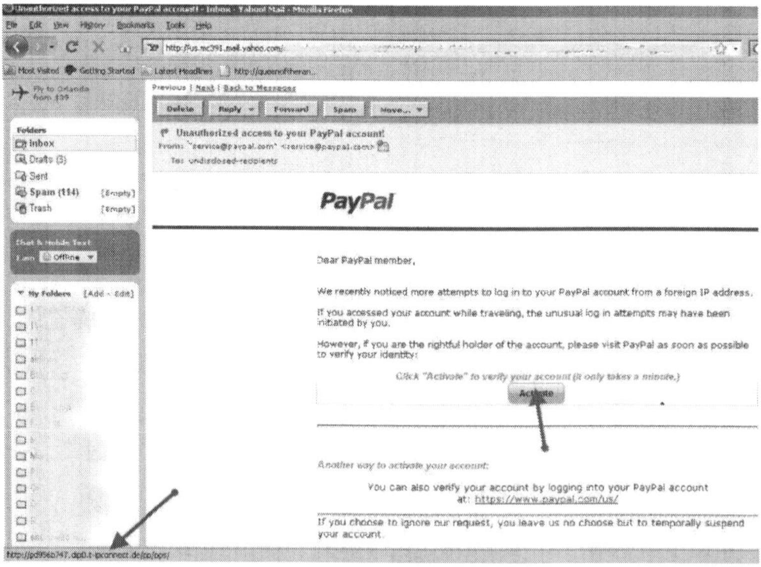

PayPal Image #2

How I Knew It Was a Scam

- The return e-mail address is service@paypaI.com (they used a capital "i" instead of an "L").
- When I moused over the "activate" button, the link actually reads **http://pd956b747.dip0.t-ipconnect.de/pp/pps/,** which means the domain is actually .de, and therefore belonging to Germany.
- This is one of the oldest phishing scams in the book.

EXAMPLE #5: Someone from eBay is Contacting Me about My Listing

In this example, I receive an e-mail from a prospective buyer about a listing I supposedly have on eBay. The listing is for a 1946 Pontiac Door Edge Mirrors, not that it matters much.

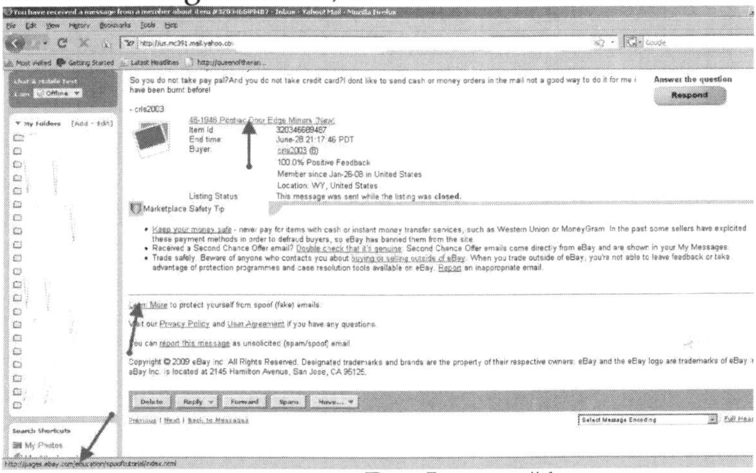

eBay Image #1

What Made It Almost Feel Real

- The images are eBay's real logos (seen on eBay Image #2)
- The layout is exactly how eBay's correspondence looks.
- When I mouse over some of the links, they go to the eBay site. In this image, I'm mousing over "Learn more to protect yourself from spoof (fake) e-mails," and the link goes to **http://pages.ebay.com/eduation/spooftutorial/index.html,** which is the actual eBay page for spoof information.

- I'm completely paranoid that my eBay account will somehow be hijacked and someone will start posting fake listings under my name. (It happened to a friend of mine.)

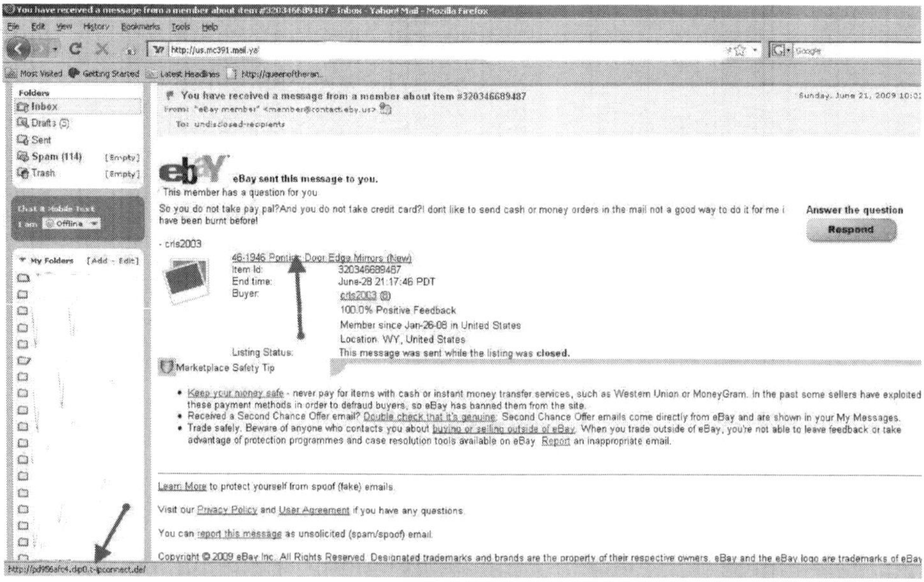

eBay image #2

How I Knew It Was a Scam

- This is another really common phishing scam.
- I have never owned a pair of Pontiac door mirrors in my life
- The e-mail was supposedly sent after the listing was closed. But the closing date was June 28, and I received the e-mail on June 21.
- The return e-mail address is **member@contact.eby.us**: they left out the "a" in eBay!
- When I mouse over the link for the Pontiac doors, I see that it actually goes to **http://pd956afc4.dp0.t-ipconnect.de** and, as we've all learned by now, the .de extension is for people in Germany!

EXAMPLE #6: Bank of America Wants to Make Sure My Account Is Secure

This e-mail is from "Bank of America." They're concerned with the "unusual number of invalid logins attempts" on my account, and want to verify that I'm really me. They'd like me to click on the link to update my account information.

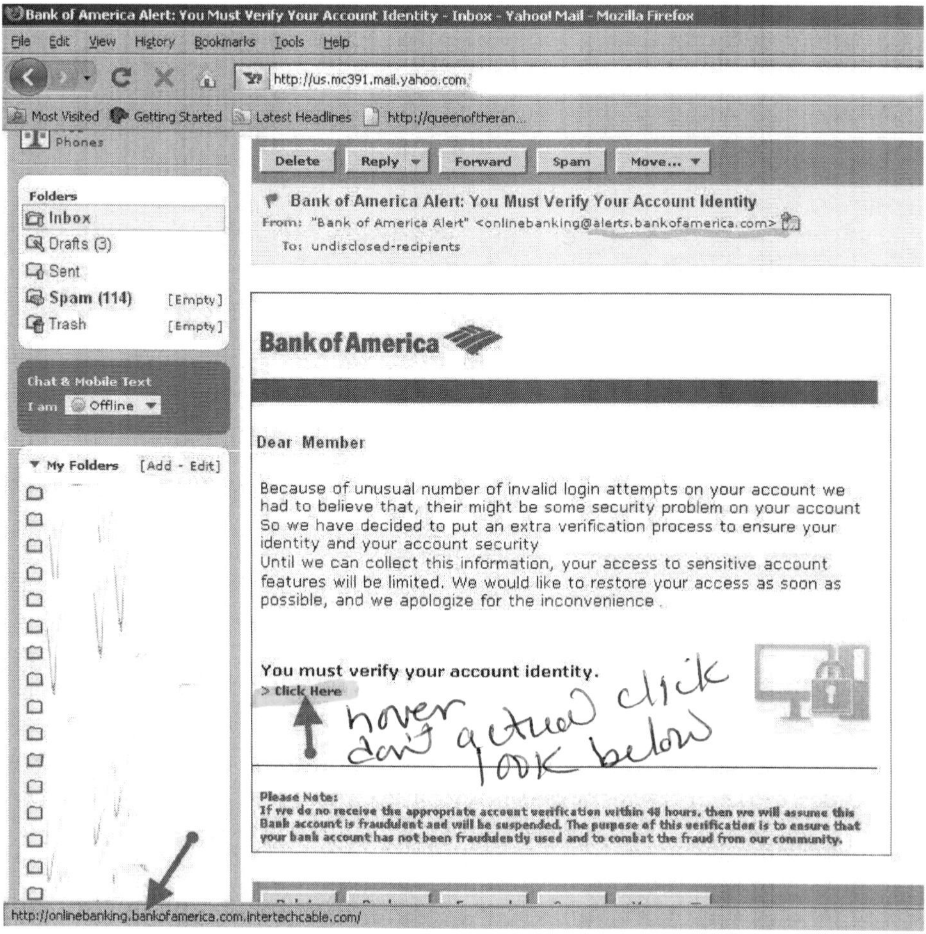

What Made It Almost Feel Real

- The images are Bank of America's real logos.
- The e-mail address appears to be from B of A: onlinebanking@alerts.bankofamerica.com.

How I Knew It Was a Scam

- I moused over the link and saw **http://onlinebanking.bankofamerica.com.intertechcable.com,** which means the real domain is intertechable.com.

- When I viewed the full headers, and looked up the IP address in ARIN.net, I saw that the originating IP was in Africa.
- Oh, and I don't have a Bank of America account!

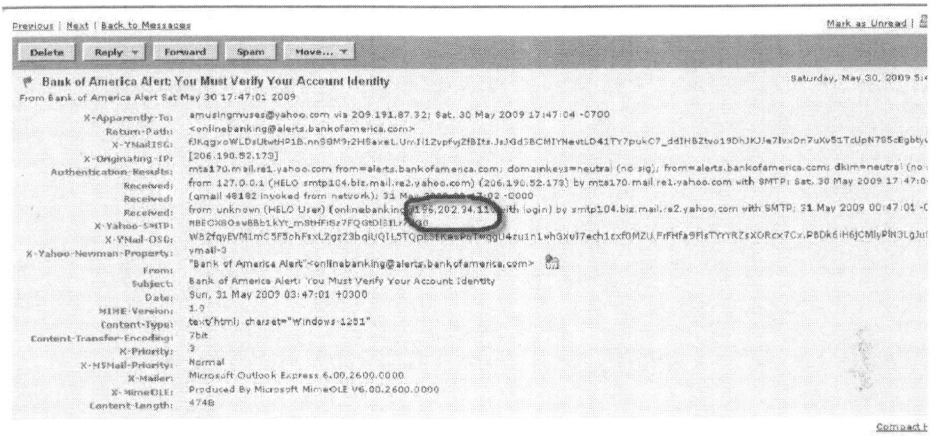

This image shows the full headers of the e-mail I received from "Bank of America." I took one of the IP addresses and went to **www.arin.net** to see where it originated. (Image on next page.)

Lo and behold, that particular IP address was assigned to the African Network Information Center. Keep in mind that this does not mean the African Network Information Center sent the e-mail. It just means that one of its customers sent it.

I wish that tracking IPs was an exact science, but sometimes you will run into some snags. Gmail's e-mails will always show Gmail, and some free accounts like Yahoo and Hotmail won't give much help either. Just keep in mind that while this can prove informative, it is not foolproof!

Looking up the IP address in ARIN.net

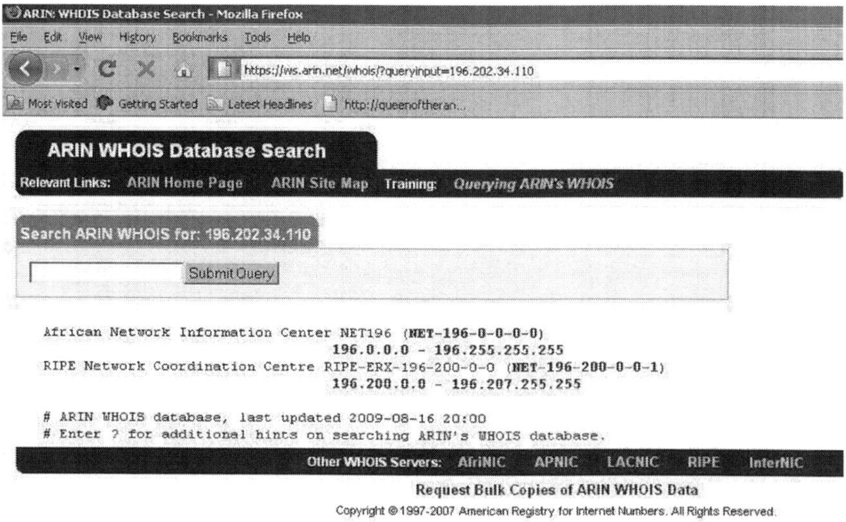

EXAMPLE #7: A Company Wants Me to Be a Mystery Shopper!

Oh, joy of joys! How I love mystery shopping and finding new companies to work for! I saw an ad on Craigslist for a company looking for new shoppers, and of course I had to check it out!

YOUR MYSTERY SHOPPER POSITION !!! Monday, May 4, 2009 12:26 AM
From: "Excel Mystery Shopper" <excelmysteryshopper@live.com>
To: amusingmuses@yahoo.com

Dear Applicant,

We got your resume and your application for the job of mystery shopper as posted on craigslist.We are global leader in Customer Experience Management. Our proven experience and systems use information from a variety of sources, including mystery shop visits and store audits to quantify the gap between your brand promise and the reality of exactly what your customers have experienced.

Eat out for free

Get paid to shop for some of your favourite brands

Become a member of a global mystery shopping network and have the opportunity to 'Shop the World!'

Help improve customer service in your local area.

Examples of details you would forward to us are after your shopping experience are:
1) How long it took you to get services.
2) Smartness of the attendant
3) Customer service professionalism
4) Sometimes you might be required to upset the attendant to see how they react to clients when they get tensed (under pressure).

We turn the information (you gave us) over to the company executives and they would carry out their own duties in improving their services. Most companies employ our assistance when people give complaints about their services or when they feel there are needs for them to improve their customer service. Your Identity would be kept confidential as the job states (secret shopper). You would be paid $100 for every survey you carry out ,bonus on your transportation allowance and funds would be given to you if you have to dine as part of the duty.
Your job will be to evaluate and comment on customer service in a wide variety of shops, stores, restaurant and services in your area. No commitment is made on this job and you would have flexible hours as it suits you. If you are interested do send in your:

(I)Your Full Name:
(II)Your Residence address:
City:
State:
Zip Code:
(III)Present work address:
(IV)Home and mobile Phone numbers:
(V)Email address:
(VI)Your Age and Current Occupation:
(VII)Your Gender:

So we can look at your distance from the locations which you have to put your service into, and your address would also be needed for your payments. We also implore you to send a scanned copy of any form of Identification for the processing of your application form and also for record purpose but if you cannot provide it presently then you can provide it later..
Thanks.

Hiring Manager
Service Research Corporation
Tom Kenneth
Tel: (850) 260-0469
Fax: (850) 260-0468

> Date: Fri, 1 May 2009 11:54:27 -0700
> From: amusingmuses@yahoo.com
> Subject: re: mystery shopping
> To: excelmysteryshopper@live.com
>
>
> Hi!
>
> I'm interested in being a mystery shopper for your company. Please let me know how to apply for your company!
>
> Thanks!
>
> -Bethany
>

What Made It Almost Feel Real

- They give a lot of information in this e-mail.
- There is a real mystery shopping company called Service Research Corporation.
- A company name, phone number, and contact person were provided.

How I Knew It Was a Scam

- The e-mail is from a free account, live.com (owned by Microsoft).
- The phone number area code is in Florida, but the writer of the ad uses British spelling and calls a cell phone a "mobile" phone.
- They asked for gender and age on the application. That's illegal in the U.S.!
- The pay is $100 per survey. Most mystery shopping assignments are $10–40.
- When I Google the phone number 850-260-0469, a **www.ripoffreport.com** listing comes up.
- I've been mystery shopping since 1999 and know companies don't advertise on Craigslist!
- I went to the *real* Service Research Corporation's website (just by Googling the name) and saw that they have warnings about fake ads on Yahoo and Craigslist.
- When I viewed the full headers and looked them up on **www.ARIN.net**, I saw that the e-mail originated from Africa.

Viewing Full Headers of Mystery Shopping E-mail

YOUR MYSTERY SHOPPER POSITION !!!

From Excel Mystery Shopper Mon May 4 00:26:32 2009

X-Apparently-To:	amusingmuses@yahoo.com via 209.191.87.32; Mon, 04 May 2009 00:26:39 -(
Return-Path:	<excelmysteryshopper@live.com>
X-YahooFilteredBulk:	65.55.111.172
X-YMailISG:	M87g4ucWLDtuKo1z.QrJYHQcKwizqo8i1YvKoYaXUTkakYObIMsreWVEoG5bt4mVA
X-Originating-IP:	[65.55.111.172]
Authentication-Results:	mta163.mail.re4.yahoo.com from=live.com; domainkeys=neutral (no sig); fron
Received:	from 65.55.111.172 (EHLO blu0-omc4-s33.blu0.hotmail.com) (65.55.111.172)
Received:	from BLU148-W11 ([65.55.111.135]) by blu0-omc4-s33.blu0.hotmail.com with
Message-ID:	<BLU148-W11EB1ECAE891F655EB26DBCA680@phx.gbl>
Return-Path:	excelmysteryshopper@live.com
Content-Type:	multipart/alternative; boundary="_652f0ec2-6bd2-4725-9d64-67acbf97cffe_"
X-Originating-IP:	[41.219.192.234]
From:	Excel Mystery Shopper <excelmysteryshopper@live.com>
To:	<amusingmuses@yahoo.com>
Subject:	YOUR MYSTERY SHOPPER POSITION !!!
Date:	Mon, 4 May 2009 00:26:32 -0700
Importance:	Normal
In-Reply-To:	<541281.24908.qm@web39102.mail.mud.yahoo.com>
References:	<541281.24908.qm@web39102.mail.mud.yahoo.com>
MIME-Version:	1.0
X-OriginalArrivalTime:	04 May 2009 07:26:32.0166 (UTC) FILETIME=[A5D69860:01C9CC89]
Content-Length:	6918

ARIN.net Listing of IP address from Mystery Shopping E-mail

ARIN WHOIS Database Search

Relevant Links: ARIN Home Page ARIN Site Map Training: *Querying ARIN's WHOIS*

Search ARIN WHOIS for: 41.219.192.234

Submit Query

```
OrgName:    African Network Information Center
OrgID:      AFRINIC
Address:    03B3 - 3rd Floor - Ebene Cyber Tower
Address:    Cyber City
Address:    Ebene
Address:    Mauritius
City:       Ebene
StateProv:
PostalCode: 0001
Country:    MU

ReferralServer: whois://whois.afrinic.net

NetRange:   41.0.0.0 - 41.255.255.255
CIDR:       41.0.0.0/8
NetName:    NET41
NetHandle:  NET-41-0-0-0-1
Parent:
NetType:    Allocated to AfriNIC
NameServer: NS1.AFRINIC.NET
NameServer: NS-SEC.RIPE.NET
NameServer: NS2.LACNIC.NET
NameServer: TINNIE.ARIN.NET
NameServer: SEC1.APNIC.NET
NameServer: SEC3.APNIC.NET
Comment:
```

Look at that! It's our good old friends at the African Network Information Center. How nice of it to send us another scammy e-mail!

Chapter 10
Reporting Scams to the Proper Authorities

If you've been scammed, it's understandable that you may feel embarrassed, or annoyed, or just plain silly because you feel like you should have known better. However, WE NEED YOU to report scams so that others don't fall into a similar fate. Don't just moan and groan on anonymous message boards, make sure you contact the right organizations so that these scams become ingrained in the public psyche. Knowing the scams out there, and how to avoid them, should be as common as looking both ways to cross the street. That can't happen unless you're willing to speak out.

Make sure that you keep records of any conversations or e-mails that happen between you and the company. Keep receipts of purchases and remember that you can seek fraud protection through your credit or debit card company. If you send documents, do it through certified mail and get a return receipt. Send copies of important documents, and keep the originals.

If you are a victim (or have successfully thwarted a feeble attempt) of a scam through a phishing e-mail, contact the company that the phisher was posing as. For example, if you received an e-mail from someone posing as Bank of America, Amazon, Wal-Mart, eBay, etc., contact that specific company. All of these large-name retailers have specific fraud departments with really smart lawyers who will handle your e-mail. Make sure to forward the complete e-mail, WITH FULL HEADERS, so that they can track the IP address. Usually these companies have specific e-mail address to contact them like **fraud@amazon.com**, or **spoof@ebay.com**, so look on their site to see where to send the information.

If a company has defrauded you (that is, not delivered goods or services as promised, it doesn't necessarily need to be a typical scam) you need to file a complaint with the region of the Better Business Bureau in which the company is located (**www.bbb.org**). Be prepared! The BBB requires that you have documented proof that you first tried to solve your difference with the company before contacting them, and it does take several weeks to get the issue resolved, but at least you'll have someone on your side!

If the scam involved postal services or mail in any way, contact the U.S. Postal Service at **www.postalinspectors.uspis.gov.** For example, someone might have stolen your mail for your credit card offers, or you might have received chain letters through the mail, or requests for charitable contributions. Likewise, the bills you send in the mail may have been taken and the checks washed to write bigger and better checks. If any of these types of things happen to you, the USPS is the one to contact.

For Internet scams, you can file a complaint through the Internet Crime Compliant Center (**www.ic3.gov**). This agency may not help with individual cases, but compile complaints to determine a pattern.

You can also file complaints through your state's Attorney General Office and through the Federal Trade Commission. Again, these agencies may not be able to help you individually, but look for patterns in complaints to build cases against offenders.

To find your Attorney General: **www.naag.org/contact.php**
FTC Complaint form: **www.ftccomplaintassistant.gov**

Part II

Making Money

Chapter 11
Quick Ways to Fast Cash

I'm guessing that this book made its way into your hands because you're looking for ways to supplement your income, or at least make ends meet until you can get your next full-time gig. Over the next several pages I'll go over random ways to make money or get cash quick. Being that I'm based in Seattle, some of these sites may not be national yet. Many new companies advertise on Craigslist job listings to get the word out. Remember to use the SCRAM principles to evaluate any listing and thoroughly research the company before signing up.

Throughout this section you'll see things that are common sense (i.e., selling your stuff on eBay) and other things you may not have considered like bartering or peer-to-peer lending.

Depending on what strikes a chord with you, you might be required to get a business license, be hired as a 1099 independent contractor, or as an employee (rare, but it could happen). Some of these ideas will require you to market yourself, so be sure to check out Part IV of this book which goes over valuable resources in starting and growing your business. Bottom line: these are ideas to get you started…you still may have some research to do on your own!

Making Money with Stuff Cluttering Your Life

Consignment Stores, Craigslist, eBay, Amazon, and Garage Sales (in that order)

Consignment stores. If you have really nice furniture or clothing, look into consignment stores in your area. I personally am not a fan of pawnshops just because they don't really give enough for your items. In my experience, consignment stores, those paying you when the item sells, are a much better deal. Each store operates differently, so check around to see what the standards are in your area.

Craigslist.com is a wonderful place to buy and sell a whole bunch of stuff. Unlike eBay and Amazon, there are no fees to list items. If I have larger items to sell, furniture, computers, electronics, vehicles, etc., I start with Craigslist. Items stay online for seven days, and you can upload four pictures. You can also go to the "free" section of Craigslist and pick up items that you think you can turn around for a profit! The best success I've had is with listing items at 6 a.m. on a Saturday morning. By Sunday evening, everything is usually gone. Keep in mind that people are expecting to pay more garage-sale prices with things listed on Craigslist so they might want to haggle. I always list my items a few dollars higher than what I really want to sell for, just in case someone wants to feel like they got a good deal. A word of safety: don't sell high-end items (like diamonds and new laptops) on Craigslist; and always meet your buyer in a public place.

eBay.com has become the standard of all online auction companies, and probably needs no introduction. You're already aware that people have sold their old clothes, trinkets, antiques, and potato chips that look like Jesus. What I have found is that Craigslist is best for larger items as well as electronics, (so people can test them out) and eBay is better for items that either need no description (like golf balls) or are somewhat unique (like a Muppet lunch-box from the 1980s). eBay does charge a per-listing fee, and shipping is always an adventure to figure out. Luckily, there are a lot of books you can borrow from the library to get you started, or just check out eBay's online tutorials.

Amazon.com has quickly gone from being a book-centered site to selling everything under the sun. If you have used items, you can list them on Amazon as well. Amazon takes a commission for the sale, so it's different from eBay in that your listing is up as long as you want it to be, and you don't pay anything unless it sells.

Half.com. Another good place to sell your used books and CDs is at Half.com. A subsidiary of eBay, Half.com specializes ONLY in media. I haven't sold anything through half.com, but I have purchased plenty of merchandise through it.

Buymytronics.com, Yourenew.com, Nextworth.com, and **Gazelle.com.** If you have old electronics that you want to get rid of, even if they're broken, check out these sites. Sometimes you'll get trade, gift certificates, or cold, hard cash.

Have a garage sale! Once you've gone through the major online resources to sell your stuff, the next step with the leftovers is to have a good, old-fashioned garage sale. Get the kids to make cookies and lemonade for more profits. If you have some technical skills, create a quick website and advertise it so people will see what kind of items you have for sale. You can also list and browse garage sales on Craigslist.

DONATE! If not everything sells after the garage sale, consider donating it to Goodwill, The Salvation Army, Purple Heart, or another charity organization. Even if you're not able to sell something, tax write-offs can still be a saving grace come April 15.

Making Money with Your Space and Physical Assets

Roommates or house-guests. If you have extra room in your house, consider getting a roommate! Many people who come into a new town need a place to crash for a few days while they're getting situated. You can offer a room, or even just a couch, and make extra money while helping someone avoid the high costs of hotel rentals. **Craigslist.com, Airbnb.com, vrbo.com** and **sublet.com** are excellent places to list your space.

Airport parking. I have a friend who lives near the Seattle Airport and has room at her house for about five cars. People will drive to her house to park, and she'll take them to the airport. She charges $5 per day, and roundtrip pick up and drop off at the gate! If you live near an airport, or even a popular area, (like stadiums for ballgames, concerts, fairs, and such) consider offering this type of service.

Your car. If you have a vehicle that you don't use that much, consider listing it on **relayrides.com.** Other people will get the wheels they need, and you can make some extra money.

Garages. Artists, musicians, amateur mechanics, and people traveling for months on end need extra space to store their stuff, create and build. If you have an extra garage or shed, consider renting it out like a storage unit.

Storage lockers. Many people need extra space, especially in apartment buildings. If you're not using your storage unit, offer it to others at your complex to see if you can make some extra cash or consider listing it on **stowthat.com**.

Parking spaces. I see ads on Craigslist all the time for people who need a place to park their RV for the winter or just an extended period of time. Likewise, if you live in an apartment or condo community that has limited parking, you can rent out your assigned space to other residents!

Your plasma. You can earn sometimes $20–$100 just by donating your plasma. Not only will you make some quick extra cash, you could potentially be saving a life as well. Check out **www.pptaglobal.org** to find a local center near you.

Hair. Many people have turned to selling their hair to make some extra cash as well. Human hair is used in extensions and wigs, and if your hair is healthy, you could fetch a pretty good price for it. Keep in mind you'll need to have at least 8-10 inches of healthy, unprocessed, un-dyed hair. This is because not all hair is the same length, so buyers want more since a lot of it may not be usable. Check out **www.hairwork.com**, **OnlineHairAffair.com,** and **www.BuyandSellHair.com** for more information.

Reproductive assets. Men can earn money by donating their sperm through local sperm banks, and women between 18 and 30 can also earn income by donating their eggs to infertile couples. Check out the local laws and regulations in your area to see what the process is for these types of donations.

Health. You can also become a Medical Trial participant and earn money by allowing yourself to be a guinea pig in drug studies. Visit **www.nimh.nih.gov** and click on "clinical trials" to see government sponsored research studies that are being conducted nationwide. You can also Google, "medical test volunteers" for more information or sign up for a free account at **www.clinicalconnection.com.**

Making Money with Domestic and Labor Gigs

These ideas can be implemented as random jobs that you can do with a company, or on your own by posting and/or answering a few ads. If you're feeling entrepreneurial, you can take it to the next level by creating a whole business. You'll just need to establish clientele and hire workers once it gets too much to be just you. (See Part IV for more information about creating a business and marketing.) Other ideas along these lines include the following:

- Personal chef
- Personal shopper
- Lawn and yard care
- Seasonal house cleaning
- House painting
- Car maintenance
- Birthday and party planning
- Home organizer
- Moving assistance

Babysitting. Find gigs in your local newspaper, or through craigslist.org. There are also many websites now that allow potential babysitters to create profiles. Some are free, some have the babysitter pay a fee to be listed, and some have the family pay a fee to view potential sitters. Examples include **www.sittercity.com, www.phoneababysitter.com**, and **www.seekingsitters.com.**

Elderly care giving. Many people live away from their aging parents and need to make sure that they're taken care of. Some may need more supervision with taking pills and getting to the doctor, but many situations could need a companion to help pass the time. Find gigs in your local newspaper, check around retirement communities, or through Craigslist.

Dog walking or pet care. I love the guilt of yuppies. They work too much and don't feel like they're home enough to take Fido for a walk, or make sure that Fifi has enough food. Many cities already have plenty of dog walking companies that you can work for. You can contact them directly, or place some ads of your own in local pet stores and around parks. Examples include: **Rover.com, Fetchpetcare.com** and **Gdaypetcare.com**.

Housecleaning. People will always need help having their house cleaned. Don't fool yourself, though, this is backbreaking hard work. Find gigs in your local job boards, through Craigslist, post your own or find an established company to work for.

Handyman/labor gigs. You can fix leaky faucets, mow lawns, clean out gutters, small home repairs, or even hanging/taking down holiday decorations. Again, local job boards and Craigslist are great resources.

Personal assistant. This involves helping a family or small businessperson out with domestic chores like doing laundry, making dinner, etc. Local job boards and Craigslist are great resources for these types of jobs. Some can be scams, however, so be sure that you meet the people in person!

Housesitting. Now that so many homes are vacant due to the housing bust (I personally know five people who have two homes, and not because they want to!) people need someone to take care of the home and make sure it's ready for showing potential buyers. Likewise, when people go on vacation, or are out of town a lot, they need someone to check in on the pets, get the mail, and water the plants. Besides your local resources, you can visit **nomador.com, trustedhousesitters.com, mindmyhouse.com,** and **luxuryhousesitting.com** for listings.

Making Money with Your Amazing Artistic Abilities

Do you have talent? Great! Create a virtual storefront for all to see and make some extra cash!

Etsy.com, Artfire.com, Artsavvy.com, Zibbet.com, and **Bonanza.com** are storefronts for artists of all genres to sell their wares. You can sell your handmade goods, materials, or vintage items. Of course, you'll need to market yourself, but it's a great way to reach an audience you may not have found before. .

CDBaby.com, bandcamp.com, Itunes.com are great places to sell your music. You'll still need to do some marketing of your own, but they'll create a searchable page for you and handle all of the payment processing and delivering of music.

The Internet has made it a lot easier for filmmakers to create and distribute (and get paid for) their films. While **YouTube.com** and **Vimeo.com** are mostly considered video hosting sites, you can also set up payment gateways as a subscription or pay-per-view. **vhx.tv** and **pivotshare.com** are two other options that will help you distribute films to a world-wide audience.

Lulu.com, LightningSource.com, and **CreateSpace.com.** These companies are geared towards self-publishers just getting started. They're print on demand (POD), and handle all of the payment processing as well. If you have a book to sell, and need to go the self-publishing route, most printers require a minimum run of 1,000 to 2,500 copies. Even if your book only costs $4 each to print, you're looking at a minimum of $4,000–$10,000 just to get started. If you're able to do some marketing on your own, POD can save you a lot of hassle until you're ready to move into larger runs. POD companies offer various ways to print your books, data and music CDs and even help with getting an IBSN, cover and layout design as well as e-book and print distribution to major bookstores and retailers.

Skreened.com, Spreadshirt.com, and **Zazzle.com** are print-on-demand companies for t-shirts, business cards, posters, calendars and other fun and unique items. You create the design, upload it to a product, and then you earn commission off of each sale of the product. They take care of payment processing, order fulfillment, returns, and merchandising. You just collect a commission check! Skreened prides itself on being socially responsible and provides sweat-shop free merchandise. My brother-in-law has been selling on Cafepress and Skreened since, well, forever, and has made consistent income from his store. You can see his shop at **http://skreened.com/irregularwear**

Cafepress.com is the king of self-created swag. If you have artistic abilities and want to see your creations on t-shirts, mugs, bags, baby-bibs, clocks, and more, Cafepress is the way to go! Each item has a set base price, and you make your profit by raising your price above the base. For example, a t-shirt could be $10, and if you set your price to $15, then you earn $5 per sale.

If you are a photographer and have a catalogue of images to sell, there are plenty of sites that can help you make an income. Beyond setting up a payment gateway for photo sharing sites like

Instagram.com, Flickr.com and **Pinterest.com**, you can license your photos to be used through **istockphoto.com, fotolia.com, dreamstime.com** and **alamy.com**.

Making Money with Your Awesome Technical Prowess

Do you have Web coding skills? Are you great with Flash or Photoshop? Can you write a killer press release? Can you edit a book or sales copy? Well, people need your skills!

There are a lot of websites that list projects for people who have skills just like you! You can make a fairly good living as a freelance graphic designer, Web designer, or coder. If you have the skills, you can make very good money helping small business owners and large corporations get the job done. The sites below may charge fees to bid on projects, or they may collect commission off of the final price of the project. Check out each one independently and see how it suits your particular needs:

- **Elance.com**
- **Flexjobs.com**
- **Freelancer.com**
- **Guru.com**
- **Odesk.com**
- **Peopleperhour.com**
- **Sologig.com**

Productionhub.com From their website: "ProductionHUB, Inc. is the global online resource and industry directory for film, television, video, live event, and digital media production. The service was developed 10 years ago as a tool for anyone with an Internet connection to locate production products, equipment, services and professionals."

MediaBistro.com works with non-creative professionals who prefer working in a creative environment. These include writers, editors, producers, publishers and others in magazine, film, TV, advertising, PR, and other media.

Writerfind.com and **Textbroker.com** cater specifically to writers and those who need writers. This includes media companies, universities, government agencies, software companies (technical writing) as well as those needing freelancers like journalists, editors, copyeditors, and PR people.

Leapforceathome.com, hires people to do internet-based research from home. You'll have to pass a comprehensive two-part exam, but there are no other fees or requirements to become a Leapforce Agent.

A note about these services: Many times you are bidding against people who are located overseas and can charge much less than you. Don't let it deter you. Many employers prefer to deal with people in their local area who can speak the native tongue. It makes communicating about the project much easier.

Making Money by Selling Other People's Stuff

Drop shipping is a retail technique in which the retailer does not keep goods in stock. When a customer order is made, the shipment details are transferred to the manufacturer or wholesaler, who then ships the goods directly to the customer. The retailer makes a profit based on the difference between the wholesale and retail price. There are many people who drop ship on eBay or sell items through PPC advertising.

www.doba.com is a large drop-shipping network with over 200 wholesale distributors, manufacturers and craftsmen. As a drop-shipper, you'll get full access to the distributors and their wholesale product catalogs.

www.salehoo.com is a wholesale directory of product suppliers for drop shipping. Their niche is primarily focused on online auctions (eBay, etc.).

Making Money by Investing

Don't let the header fool you. I am not now, nor have I ever been a Wall Street wizard. However, I do know that people can make money in the stock market, trading from home. Before you venture out and risk your life savings, keep in mind there are some other options that have come up in recent years.

Etrade.com. A traditional way of trading stocks and options through the New York Stock Exchange. You're charged a fee per trade, and sometimes maintenance fees as well.

Peer-to-peer lending. Many people are being denied for regular loans now due to the complete disarray of our banking system. To fill this need, peer-to-peer lending groups have sprung up. Investors decide on which profiles to fund, and the borrower pays back over time. Some requests are for small business loans, paying off high credit card rates, or even micro-lending to help finance a business. Keep in mind that since this is "investing" there is a risk that you may not get your money back so choose your projects carefully! If you're looking to fund your own idea, you can check out the following sites below, and refer to section IV for crowd-sourcing websites as well.

- **www.Prosper.com**
- **www.Lendingclub.com**
- **www.Zopa.com**

A Note on Crowdfunding

The sharing economy has helped many a small business owner find funds for their projects. On sites like **Kickstarter.com** and **IndieGogo.com**, you can post a project or need for funds and get small pledges to ultimately reach your goal. Due to investment laws, you may or may not be allowed to get a financial return on your monetary pledge. That is why I don't list the crowdfunding websites here. If you're looking for money to fund a business or project, go through the resource section of this book. There are a ton of niche crowdsourcing sites. One may fit your needs!

Making Money as a Market Research Participant

Market Research is where regular people give their opinions so that companies can make their products and services "new and improved." You can get fairly lucrative focus group, mock trial, and survey work through your local market research companies. They usually have postings on Craigslist's "etc." job board, and you can also do a Google search for "market research" "focus group" and your city. Remember, these people are paying YOU. You never have to pay a fee to get Market Research work!

In-Person Focus Groups last for about 1-2 hours and generally pays $50 and up. You may have a one-on-one session or be in a group. You'll be evaluating food, movies, pet products, and other various things. You can get focus group work on Craigslist, and also by contacting the Market Research companies. I'm based in Seattle, so I would feel bad if I didn't include these awesome companies:

- Fieldwork Seattle **www.fieldwork.com**
- Hartman Group **www.hartman-group.com**
- Northwest Insights **www.nwinsights.com**

Be a Mock Juror

Mock jurors help lawyers evaluate certain aspects of their case to decide whether they want to incur the expense of going to court, or just settle. You can be a mock juror in your area by contacting the large law firms and find out who conducts their mock trials. Usually, it's a market research company. You can also call up your local market research companies and ask if they do mock trials as well. If you want to do mock jury online, you can sign up for the following sites. Make sure you read through the requirements of each site before joining.

- **www.Ejury.com**
- **www.onlineverdict.com**
- **www.trialpractice.com**

Online Surveys and Focus Groups. These companies will send you surveys to fill out online or ask you to be part of a web focus group. You may earn direct cash with the surveys, or you may earn points that can be redeemed for cash or other items. **You are not going to make a lot of money doing online surveys!** It took me nearly a year to make $50 with Global Test Market, but when I finally did get that check, it was nice to have! Since these companies are constantly merging, please visit **www.BuzzyRecommends.com** for a current list of companies and resources.

Online Focus Groups

- **www.acop.com**
- **www.inboxdollars.com**
- **www.epollsurveys.com**
- **www.globaltestmarket.com**
- **www.globalopinionpanels.com**
- **www.lightspeedpanel.com**
- **www.mindfieldonline.com**
- **www.mysurvey.com**
- **www.npdor.com**
- **www.opinionoutpost.com**
- **www.pineconeresearch.com**
- **www.sendearnings.com**
- **www.specpan.com**
- **www.surveyhead.com**
- **www.surveysavvy.com**
- **www.surveyspot.com**
- **www.truepanel.com**
- **www.valuedopinions.com**
- **www.videochatnetwork.net**
- **www.zoompanel.com**

Medical Research Participant

Don't forget that you can also make money as a guinea pig for science! (Check out the earlier part of this section "Making Money with your Physical Assets" for more information.)

Making Money with Affiliate Programs

Affiliate marketing is where you promote someone else's product and earn a commission off of the sale of the product. There are many affiliate programs to choose from, and you certainly don't need to limit yourself to just one product. Before you dive into affiliate marketing, learn a little bit about the business, as you'll need to familiarize yourself with online marketing techniques. There are plenty of books and websites devoted to affiliate marketing, one of my favorites being the Warrior Forum, where Internet marketers gather to share information: **www.Warriorforum.com.**

Commission Junction—www.cj.com

CJ is a large network of affiliate vendors (they call publishers) like Home Depot, Hotels.com, Sony, etc. You can join on to CJ at no cost and apply to various programs. CJ charges hefty fees to its vendors to support and maintain their affiliate programs, so they offer many brand-names and large corporations.

Linkshare—www.linkshare.com

Like CJ, Linkshare is another large network of Affiliate Vendors. They offer companies like iTunes, Delta, CompUSA, Netflix, etc. Linkshare charges fees to its vendors to support and maintain its affiliate programs. As an affiliate, you can join Linkshare at no cost and apply to various programs.

Clickbank—www.clickbank.com

Clickbank is a unique affiliate network, as it deals ONLY with digital products and services. Because of this, most of its vendors are entrepreneurs and sell items like e-books, downloadable software, and subscription services. Clickbank is extremely well-known in the affiliate marketing world, and it's where I am listed for my products as well!

Don't forget about the little guy!

Not all businesses are listed in these types of networks and directories. If there is a company or product that you would like to promote, check around their website to see if they offer an in-house affiliate program. Usually there is an "affiliates" link, or you can just e-mail them for more information. You can also check out **www.buzzyrecommends.com** for my recommendations of affiliate program resources and trainings.

Making Money with Writing

We have moved into the information age with the Internet being a cornerstone of our daily existence. Because of this, *Writers Rule the Web!* There are a ton of businesses and individuals who need help writing and expressing their messages online. "Content creators" are needed to blog, write, or even create videos to make sure that a website constantly has content.

Put your English degree to work! Here are some ideas and sites to help you get started:

Search Engine Optimization Content Creator

Don't be scared by the fancy title; these people write the words that appear on a company's website that help drive traffic to them. Websites need to be dynamic nowadays, and constantly have to have new information. You write the words that appear on a company's website, and gear them so that they're search engine friendly and more people will find them. You'll need to learn a little about SEO (search engine optimization, which means getting to the top of search engine results for your industry) and find the companies that need help in boosting their online profile, but if you can secure a few clients, you'll have steady income. You can find this work through **elance.com**, **freelancer.com** and other sites in the "Making Money with your Awesome Technical Prowess" section.

Blogging for Yourself or Others

If you have your own blog you can sell advertising on it, promote Google's Adsense, or link to affiliate programs. Your blog doesn't have to be anything particularly fancy or deep and meaningful. Blogs like **www.cakewrecks.com** and **www.icanhascheezburger.com** are silly, light-hearted and bring in revenue. Just focus on what you love, what interests you, and people will naturally find you. It will also help if you get some good books and browse websites about blogging.

Blogging for others doesn't create as much revenue. It seems as though everyone and their brother is trying to start an online blog and want "volunteer" or "intern" bloggers. If you can find a company that pays you to blog, expect to be paid per view, or a flat rate (like \$1–\$5) for your post. You can find job postings for bloggers at **http://jobs.problogger.net.**

If you have a blog or website you can earn revenue when you review products. Just remember that the FTC now requires you to be up-front if you're being paid to review products in exchange for income or other rewards. Visit these sites for information:
FTC document, "Dot Com Disclosures": **http://bit.ly/rKUJIh**
FTC endorsement guide: **http://1.usa.gov/w1FYI**

In addition to these sites, check out the sections of this book titled: "Making Money with your Technical Prowess" and "Making Money with Micro Gigs." Many people use those sites to post needs for writers and proofreaders as well.

- **www.blogburner.com**
- **www.bloggerwave.com**
- **www.bloggingads.com**
- **www.blogitive.com**
- **www.blogsvertise.com**
- **www.linkworth.com**
- **www.loudlaunch.com**
- **www.payperpost.com**
- **www.payu2blog.com**
- **www.reviewme.com**
- **www.smorty.com**
- **www.sponsoredreviews.com**

Sites that will pay you for content (writing, blogging, and video)

- **www.about.com**
- **www.blip.tv** (video too)
- **www.constant-content.com**
- **www.creative-weblogging.com**
- **www.digitaljournal.com**
- **www.ehow.com (**video too)
- **www.examiner.com**
- **www.factoidz.com**

- **www.helium.com**
- **www.howcast.com** (video too)
- **www.myessays.com**
- **www.suite101.com**

Proofreading and editing jobs:

- **www.cyberedit.com**
- **www.editfast.com**
- **www.proofreadnow.com**

Making Money With "Get Paid To" Companies

In an earlier section of this book, I promised to list some of the companies that do actually pay you to try out products. I hesitate in listing them only because this is NOT consistent income, and frankly, it's not a lot of money either. However, they do exist, and if you want to try them out to make a little extra money here and there, have at it.

Get Paid to Try

I'm not a big fan of these. Remember, you're only making money because you sign up for an offer and get a rebate. If you don't cancel your free trial (usually 30 days) you will be billed their monthly rate. Make sure you stay on top of those cancelation dates!

- **www.cashcrate.com**
- **www.mypoints.com**
- **www.Squishycash.com**

Get Paid to Drive

I met a retired couple who spent the majority of their summer shuttling RVs back and forth to various dealerships through **www.RVtransport.com**. You can also visit your local dealerships and see if they're looking for people to transport their inventory.

If you have a commute among popular roadways and log a ton of mileage running errands, you can also place ads on your car to earn extra income through **www.Drivenmediaonline.com** and **www.MyFreeCar.com**.

Uber.com, lyft.me, sidecar.cr are all disrupting the taxicab model. Using their apps on your smart phone, you can pick up drivers and shuttle them to the airport, bank, grocery store, nightclub, or wherever else they want to go. Not all companies are in all cities, though, and of course, the taxi industry is trying to crack down on the practice. But if you have spare time, and a newer car (2000 or 2005 model or newer, depending on company requirements) then you can make some extra money.

Get Paid to Receive Mail

There is a lot of money in the direct mail business, (think catalogues and ads and such) and so mail decoy agents are used to verify that these mailings are received. Mass mailers will combine real physical addresses from decoys (that's you) but with a fake name to create a special record in their mailing list. When you receive the mail at your address (but with the fake name) you submit information from the mail that you receive. This service is also used to trace the theft of mailing lists! All bulk mailers use decoys to see how their mailings end up.

- **www.Hausernet.com**
- **www.usmonitor.com/agentform**

Making Money with Micro-Gigs

Mturk.com. Amazon's Mechanical Turk program is where companies post tasks that machines cannot easily do, but that are relatively simple for humans. For example: converting a flash-based website into text. You can choose an assignment, and, on completion, are credited with payment to your Amazon account.

Fiverr.com. Born out of the recession, Fiverr asks people what they will do for $5. It could be editing a resume, being your Facebook friend, or anything in-between!

GigWalk.com Businesses will publish gigs to be completed by individuals on their own schedule.

MyCheapJobs.com and Gigbucks.com are similar to Fiverr, in that people will post what they can do, (or what they need) but aren't restricted by the $5 price point. **TaskRabbit.com** has the same philosophy, but is geared to more in-person gigs like dog walking or picking up dry cleaning. **Agentanything.com** is for college students to complete tasks, and while **Zaarly.com** started out as a random job site, it has now morphed into being specifically for the home service expert: house cleaners and gardening work.

Trade for What You Really Need

A lot of the time, we need money to buy stuff. If your wallet is in a pinch, consider the power of trade and barter. There are hundreds of groups out there that will allow you to swap books, DVDs, clothes, furniture, baby items and more. If you have a business to run, there are bartering clubs so you can trade for services like website design, marketing, massage, or even haircuts!

Don't forget about your own community—you can always have a "trading party" with friends. Have them bring old clothes, house wares, baby stuff, and just trade your little hearts out!

Trade, Bartering and Free Stuff

- **www.Craigslist.org** (click on "Free" or "Barter")
- **www.favorpals.com**
- **www.freecycle.org**
- **www.tradeaway.com**
- **www.trashbank.com**

Business Bartering (although not necessarily exclusively)

- **www.bizx.com**
- **www.itex.com**
- **www.u-exchange.com/businessbarter**

Swapping Books, CDs, DVDs, and Video Games

- **www.bookmooch.com**
- **www.paperbackswap.com**
- **www.swapacd.com**
- **www.swapadvd.com**
- **www.swaptree.com**
- **www.titletrader.com**
- **www.whatsonmybookshelf.com**

Swapping Baby Goods

- **www.handmedowns.com**
- **www.swapbabygoods.com**
- **www.thredup.com**

Swapping Clothing and Accessories

- **www.dignswap.com**
- **www.makeupalley.com**
- **www.swapstyle.com**

Swapping Homestays and Accommodations

- **www.couchsurfing.com**
- **www.digsville.com**
- **www.globalfreeloaders.com**
- **www.homebase-hols.com**
- **www.homeexchange.com**
- **www.homelink.org**

Part III

Get a Random Job

Chapter 12
Extra Money as an Employee or Independent Contractor

Maybe you're not quite ready to put in the effort of running your own business and trying to find clients and customers, and you'd rather work for someone else but not in a traditional setting. Luckily, there is a lot of opportunity for you as well! This section dives into companies that hire people (either as employees or independent contractors) to do work with flexible hours. Some may require you to work at specific sites, but many are ok with you telecommuting from home.

Before we get into all of that, however, I do recommend that you check out Part IV of this book: "Becoming the Ultimate Business Professional" before you head out on your job hunt. There you'll learn what it means to be an Independent Contractor, tips for marketing yourself and applying to jobs.

Get a Random Job using Craigslist.org

Even with the influx of Micro-Gig websites, Craigslist is still my website of choice for finding random gigs and money-making opportunities in my local area. In time, I'm sure the reach of the micro-gig sites will spread more nationally, but for now, it can be spotty depending on where you live. Plus, other job boards like **Monster.com, CareerBuilder.com** or **Indeed.com** simply don't have the variety of flexible work available since they are geared toward traditional employment.

In most cities, posting a listing on Craigslist is absolutely free. This is why it attracts spammers and scammers in droves. The two main areas to look for work on Craigslist are on the main job board and in the "gigs" section.

If you're not familiar with Craigslist, the layout of each city's site looks like this:

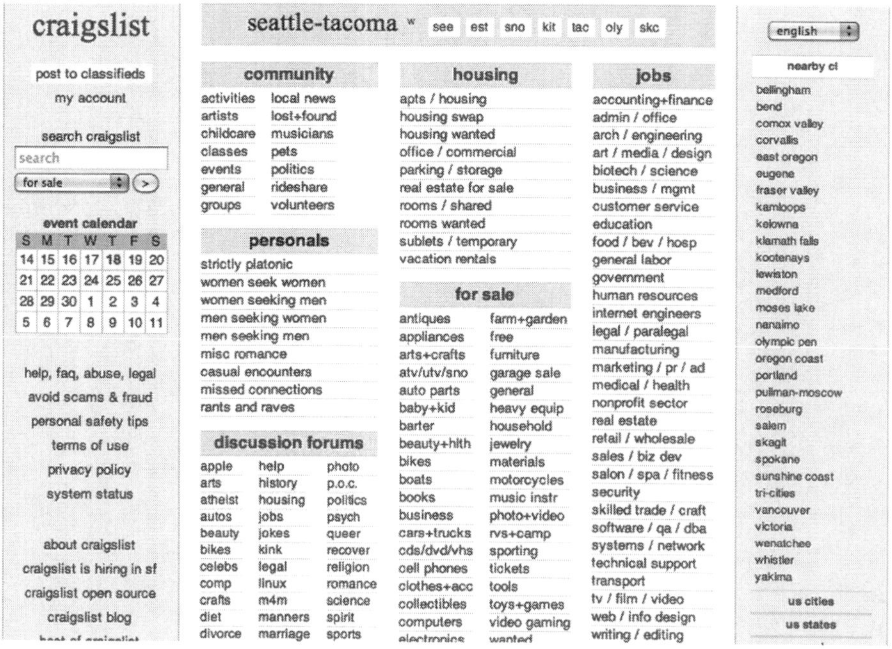

In the mid-right corner is the "jobs" board. This is where you're going to find the most legitimate work. Some cities require that a job poster pay a one-time fee (usually $20–$50) to post in that area. Those particular job boards are definitely more legitimate than the ones that don't require a fee. After all, spammers don't want to have to shell out hundreds of dollars to get their message out there—they'd rather stick to the free listings.

All the way at the bottom of the "job" column is my favorite category, "ETC." Here is where a lot of random things (like focus groups and surveys) are posted. Remember, since it's in the "job" column, these may be paid listings.

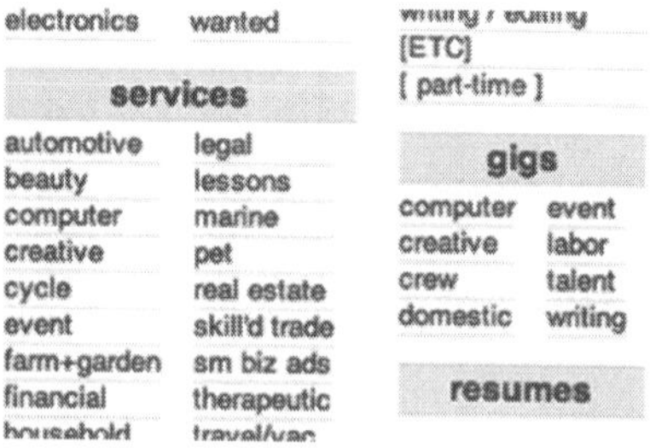

However, if you look just below the "Job" column, there is a shorter column called "gigs." The "gig" listings are always free to post, which also means that they can be a little sketchy or random.

Just remember to look at each listing (paid or not) with a critical eye and follow the SCRAM steps outlined earlier to determine if they're scams or not.

Examples of work I have done include the following:

- Transcribed notes for budding author's book
- Bought books through a massive library sale for an Amazon bookseller
- Took photographs of foreclosed homes for real estate investors
- Assisted in crafting wedding invitations
- Modeled for a tarot card calendar
- Helped cart away trash to the dump
- Installed a program for a small business's website
- Participated in a focus group about pets
- Distributed flyers door to door for a painting company
- Worked as a character actress for a fundraiser

Get a Random Job using Temp Agencies

If you're in the need for some money and don't want to waste time contacting every ad you see in the help-wanted section in hopes of getting an interview, contact a temp agency! They specialize in weird, random jobs that could become more permanent, or are specifically a one-day gig.

Some temp agencies specialize in specific skill-sets like accounting, biology/science, office work, and others. You can find temp agencies by searching "Temp Agency" or "Employment Agency" and your city. You can also look at **www.rateatemp.com** for a fairly comprehensive listing of temp agencies with ratings from people who worked there.

Nationwide agencies include the following:

- Kelly Services—**www.kellyservices.com**
- Labor Ready—**www.laborready.com**

- Manpower—**www.manpower.com**

Get a Random Job Delivering...

If you have reliable transportation a whole host of delivery type jobs are available to you. I personally have delivered phone books and hotel brochures. Don't forget you can always work for a taxi or limo service in your spare time as well. These jobs are a little more flexible.

Phone books. It is required by law that each residence gets a phone directory. And while that means we usually end up with an extra trip to the recycling bin, you can earn some money in your spare time! Contact the Yellow Pages (**www.yellowpages.com**) and the Yellow Book (**www.yellowbook.com**) for hiring information.

Hotel brochures. You know all of those brochures in the lobby? Well, they need to be stacked by someone! Each hotel is different, (some have them delivered) so just visit your local hotels and see what company they use. Contact the company to see how you can get a job delivering for them.

Newspapers and magazines. Even though paper news is slowly dying out, people are still needed to deliver newspapers, magazines, as well as free publications. Just call them up and see who's hiring.

Food/pizza. Pizza delivery is a great way to earn some extra cash. It usually pays minimum wage plus tips, but you'll need to be available in the evenings and on weekends. Many restaurants also use delivery services, and let's not leave out bakeries (wedding cakes) or even florists. Many businesses are popping up with apps that make delivering food a breeze. In Seattle we have **Munchery.com** and **Postmates.com.** You may have others in your city to explore.

Process server. This is someone who delivers legal documents to people who are getting served. It can be a pain since the person generally doesn't want to be served, so you might have to be a little sleuthy. Some states require licensing, so do your research beforehand.

Courier/bike messenger. There are a ton of companies that use couriers and bike messengers to get documents around town quickly. Generally you will be working for a courier company, and business hours are typically needed, although not necessarily.

Get a Random Job as a Merchandiser, Demonstrator, or Mystery Shopper

Merchandising

Merchandising is where you go into a store to set up displays, put out Valentine's Day cards, or check prices at a given store. It generally pays minimum wage, or a little more, and sometimes you get reimbursed for your mileages. It's a flexible way to make some extra money, and you can find this work through the "general help wanted" section of your newspaper, by looking on Craigslist under "general labor," through temp agencies, or by going to **www.RGIS.com** and **www.wisintl.com**, two companies that have merchandising assignments nationwide. You can also check out **www.worldalliance-retail.org,** which is a national organization for professional merchandising companies.

Product Demonstrator

You've seen people at the grocery store or Costco giving out free samples, right? Well you can be one of those people if you like! Product demonstration is very easy to do, generally you get a typical four- to six-hour shift during high-traffic times and are responsible for passing out foods, drinks, or other goodies. Much of this work is filled through merchandising companies, temp agencies or PR firms. Many times Craigslist is a good resource to find these jobs quickly.

Mystery Shopping

Can I just tell you how tired I am of people saying that mystery shopping is a scam? It's NOT.

I started mystery shopping in 1999, and it's been around a heckofa lot longer than that. Actually, mystery shopping got started in the 1940s (that's as far back as I could find it, anyway) people were hired to try and steal things from stores. The owners wanted to see if the employees were on their toes. People were hired to make purchases to make sure that the employee gave back correct change, closed the cash drawer, etc. Well, nowadays, we have checkpoint stands, we have security cameras, and so we don't really need that type of service. So, mystery shopping evolved into a more customer service-oriented program.

Every industry gets shopped: apartments, banks, retail stores, restaurants, movie theatres, batting cages, amusement parks, hotels, motels, resorts, cruise lines, self-storage facilities, hospitals, cell phone providers, just to name a few. As a "shopper" you will be asked to report back on how employees, products, and services are viewed by the average person. The companies can use this information to evaluate customer service, observe loss prevention methods, maintain compliance issues (alcohol and tobacco purchases), observe fair housing practices, train employees, observe potential employees and observe the competition within their industry

Mystery shopping in my opinion is one of the best part-time gigs out there. You'll need to have reliable transportation and decent writing skills, but you can get paid for giving your opinion on products and services you receive. I produced a two-hour training program on the ins and outs of mystery shopping, so a blurb here simply won't do it justice. For more information, visit my website at **www.QueenoftheRandomJob.com** and look for the Mystery Shopping category. There is more than enough information to get your started in mystery shopping, focus groups, mock trials, and other forms of market research. If you just want to jump right in, you can visit **www.jobslinger.com** or **www.mysteryshop.org,** but if you need guidance along the way with 200+ legitimate companies to work for, check out my Mystery Shopper Training Program available through **www.QueenoftheRandomJob.com.**

Get a Random Job as an Online Guide

Remember back in the day when we had 800 and 900 numbers to call for information, advice, and even to talk to Santa? Everything has moved online now, and you can get paid helping others with questions and problems.

Liveperson.com and **Justanswer.com.** These are sites where people pay per minute to chat or talk live to somebody about a variety of issues. It could be for technical support with computers, someone who needs help with a fashion emergency, or even religious counseling. You determine what you are an expert in, set your topics and per-minute fee. You'll be more successful at this if you market yourself, rather than wait for people to find you.

Chacha.com and **Kgbanswers.com.** Not everyone is Internet-savvy, so these sites were developed to help people search the web or find information quickly through text and mobile devices. As a guide (or agent) you'll receive requests from people to get information on just about anything.

Keen.com, Psychicjobcenter.com. If you have a talent for card reading, astrology, or are otherwise talented in the psychic arts, these companies need your help! Much like the 900 numbers of yore, people will come to the sites seeking advice, and you work your magic.

Get a Random Job Using Text

It is always my goal to provide all kinds of information about how people can make extra money in their spare time, so if this section offends you, just move on to the next page.

What kind of job would allow you to have your primary method of communication through text? Why those in the adult industry, of course! Some call these "phone acting" or "text acting" jobs, but let's face it, the adult industry is a BILLION-dollar-a-year industry, and if you are so inclined, you can get work with the following companies.

- **www.adultstaffing.com**
- **www.evokechat.co.uk (may be Europe only, not sure)**
- **www.papillonagency.com**
- **www.sexyjobs.com/workathome.asp**
- **www.text121chat.com**

Get a Random Job Providing Virtual Support

Many companies are cutting their overhead and allowing people to work from home. Because of this, a whole industry of "virtual assistants" have popped up, where the day-to-day work of an organization can be outsourced to folks like you.

You may be required to do general office work, do cold calling, take phone orders, give product tours, convince people to try a service or make a donation, work in debt collection, or just book an appointment.

You need to have basic office skills and might have to take tests in order to qualify. It may take time to get into their database, but once you get listed in these companies, you'll be considered for a vast array of work. You can also check out the International Virtual Assistants Association for more information at **www.ivaa.org.**

General Office Assistance and More

- **www.accoladesupport.com**
- **www.acddirect.com**
- **www.alpineaccess.com**
- **www.appen.com**
- **www.arise.com**
- **www.axiondata.com**
- **www.backgroundprofiles.com**
- **www.cloud10corp.com**
- **www.customloyal.com**
- **www.grindstone.com**
- **www.liveops.com**
- **www.teamdoubleclick.com**
- **www.teletech.com**
- **www.unitedvirtual.com**
- **www.virtualvocations.com**
- **www.westathome.com**
- **www.workingsol.com**

Telemarketing/Call Centers

- **www.bsgclearing.com/index.php/voicelog**
- **www.theappointmentbiz.com**

- **www.service800.com**
- **www.niteoservices.com**
- **www.myxact.com**
- **www.telereach.com**
- **www.intrep.com**
- **www.brightenemployment.com**
- **www.verafast.com**
- **www.vipdesk.com**
- Directory Assistance—You'll answer questions and provide support when people call 411 or any 555 number. Call your local phone company to inquire about jobs.

Tech Support

- **www.computerassistant.com**
- **www.geeksontime.com**
- **www.plumchoice.com**
- **www.supportfreaks.com**

Get a Random Job in the Education Field

If you have a background in education, or sometimes just a college degree, you could also get work with various companies as a tutor, test scorer, or instructor. You can even sell your lesson plans through **Teacherspayteachers.com** for residual income!

Tutoring (Online and Offline)

- **www.edufire.com**
- **www.studypoint.com**
- **www.sylvanlearning.com**
- **www.tutor.com**
- **www.tutorsource.com**
- **www.wyzant.com**

Standardized Test Scoring

- **www.measuredprogress.org**
- **www.pearsonassessments.com**

Instructing Online Classes

- **www.brainmass.com**
- **www.coursebridge.com**
- **www.ed2go.com**
- **www.giantcampus.com**
- **www.udemy.com**

Instructing Real-World Classes

Substitute teaching. Check out your local school district (and even some nearby districts) to get into its database of substitutes. You don't necessarily have to have a teaching certificate. Sometimes a college degree, (and a lot of patience,) will do.

Community education. I've been teaching my mystery shopping and work-at-home classes through community education since 2002. These types of classes are generally geared toward adults. Some are run through community colleges, others are run through the school district, but all offer wonderfully fun things like yoga, language classes, and underwater basket weaving!

Become a mad scientist. www.madscience.org is an educational company that gives lessons in science to school kids. They do all the training, and you just travel around to various schools and private parties putting on demonstrations.

Teach Your Native Language: Both Berlitz **(www.berlitz.com)** and Rosetta Stone **(www.rosettastone.com)** are internationally recognized language schools. You'll be put through rigorous training and will only be allowed to tutor your native language. Your clients could be kids, individuals looking to travel, people who got relocated to your area for a job, or their spouses.

Traffic school. People with personality are needed to teach traffic school to those just getting their licenses or if they've had too many tickets. Check around your local private traffic schools and DMV to see how the hiring process works.

Test preparation. ACT, SAT, GRE, GMAT, LSAT—all these wonderful abbreviations spell terror in many a student's heart. Teachers are needed to help prepare students to take these exams. The sites of two national companies are **www.Kaplan.com** and **www.PrincetonReview.com.**

Get a Random Job in the Health Field

Some jobs require medical knowledge and training of course, but other random jobs don't. Whether you have a medical degree or not, here are some things that you can do in the medical field:

Concierge doctor or nurse. Many doctors hate dealing with insurance companies. It takes up a lot of time resources and energy, and most of the time they don't even get reimbursed for what they bill. Concierge doctors are making a comeback; these are doctors, nurses, and skilled practitioners who make house calls and provide services at a flat fee. No involvement with insurance agencies required. Of course, you first have to go through medical school and *become* a doctor or nurse practitioner, but once that process is through, with a little marketing on your own you could run your own practice and set your own schedule.

Tissue recovery technician/organ courier. At its core, this is simply delivery work. You'll be transporting organs and tissues throughout your local area (or even country) to awaiting facilities for transplants and operations. If you mess up, however, it literally could cost lives. You can learn more about how to become a Tissue Recovery Technician at: **www.quickintl.com**

Administering drug tests. "Certified Professional Collector" is the official term used for people who administer drug tests for employment and recovery centers. Laws vary by state, but sometimes you'll need to go through training and get certified on how to collect blood, urine, hair, and skin samples for drug testing. Visit the Drug and Alcohol Testing Industry Association website for more information: **www.datia.org.**

Fonemed.com is a phone triage where nurses field calls about a wide array of issues. You can work at home in your spare time, and help people decide whether in-person medical attention is necessary.

Get a Random Job for Cops and Firefighters

Sidegig.com is a great resource and job board for those who have or had experience in law enforcement or firefighting. Some job examples include security, private investigators, and chauffeurs.

Get a Random Job as a Translator

If you speak, read, and write a foreign language fluently, then there are plenty of companies who want to hire you as a freelance translator.

- **www.accurapid.com**
- **www.languagesunlimited.com**
- **www.languagetranslation.com**
- **www.lionbridge.com**
- **www.sdl.com**
- **www.telelanguage.com**
- **www.welocalize.com**

Get a Random Job Transcribing Documents

Transcription is a highly sought-after skill within many professions. Doctors need transcribers to make physical copies of their client notes and charts. The court system needs transcribers to record sessions and depositions. Even the entertainment industry needs transcribers to close-caption videos and other media. Many community colleges offer some two- and four-year programs to complete the basics needed to learn this skill. You can get more information and a list of approved schools at **www.ahdionline.org**

More Information

American Academy of Professional Coders: **www.aapc.com**
American Medical Billing Assoc: **www.ambanet.net/AMBA.htm**

Companies that Hire Transcribers

- **www.alicedarling.com**
- **www.emediamillworks.com**
- **www.ewordsolutions.com**
- **www.execuscribe.com**
- **www.medquist.com**
- **www.nettranscripts.com**
- **www.oracletranscription.com**
- **www.precysesolutions.com**
- **www.productiontranscripts.com**

- **www.speak-write.com**
- **www.stenotran.com**
- **www.talk2type.net**
- **www.tigerfish.com**
- **www.transcription-services.org**

Get a Random Job as a Performer/Artist

Artist in Residence. Whether you are a visual or performance artist, there are artist in residence programs through local schools, colleges, and community organizations. Search for "artist in residence" as well as your city to see what is available to you. If you're feeling adventurous, you can also find artist in residence programs abroad. As a puppeteer, I have worked both through the New York and Detroit School systems as well as in Taiwan!

Children's party or corporate event performer. Clown, balloon artist, character actor, mascot, caricaturist, handwriting analyzer, party psychic, mock casino dealer, and more! There are a ton of companies in your area that provide birthday, corporate, graduate, and fundraising entertainment. I've known plenty of puppeteers, mimes, and other performers who made a decent income for just a few hours' worth of work. Contact your local companies to see how you can get work with them.

Movie extra. Extras are needed to make a movie/TV show appear more "real." They are the people in the background sipping coffee, driving cars, walking down the street, or otherwise just keeping to themselves while the main actors steal the scene. You don't need to have any kind of acting experience! The easiest way to find legitimate extra work is to contact your local film office (every city has one) and find out what projects are coming up. Then contact the agencies responsible for finding extras, and you'll earn some pretty good wages. Remember that since extra work is in the film industry, it can be union, which means it pays really well!

Voice actor. Voice talent is used not only for radio and TV promos, but also on the Web and for books on tape. Now that technology has become sophisticated, you can create a very professional sounding demo-reel right from your home computer. Visit **www.sunspotproductions.com,** **www.earworks.com,**

www.voice123.com, www.gmvoices.com, www.procommss.com, www.perfectvoices.com, and **www.mktmania.com** to get more information about submitting your demo tapes and getting work.

Busker. These are the performance artists who hang out at fairs and festivals playing instruments or performing in other ways to grasp an audience's attention. I knew a guy who used to go out in the holiday season, dressed as Santa Claus, with his ukulele and sang Christmas carols. As a busker, you're only working for tips, so keep that in mind!

Model. Models are needed for art classes, budding photographer portfolios, print publications, and more. You can contact your local art schools, colleges and universities for classroom work. If you want to go a little more professional, contact your local casting agencies to find out about print model work. Many film-casting agencies also work with print models.

Standardized patients. Do you remember the *Seinfeld* episode where Kramer was hired to act out various illnesses for student doctors? Well, that's actually a real job! As a "standardized patient," you'll be given various diseases to act out with various symptoms to help certify student doctors. Yes, you will be poked, prodded, and required to wear a hospital gown. To get this type of work, check with your local medical schools. Nearly every school uses standardized patients, so they'll be able to point you in the right direction.

Tradeshows. You don't have to be a model to get tradeshow work. People of all kinds are needed to showcase products and services, conduct demonstrations, assist in check-in, directing participants, or even just hold raffles. Contact your local convention center to see about the events coming up in your area, and to connect with the companies putting them on. Most likely, you'll be working with a marketing or promotion agency. One nearly nationwide company is Wolfpromotions.com.

Places to Find Job Listings in Entertainment

You can certainly find your own work in the entertainment world through the sites listed below. Of course, these will be little roles that may not pay that much, (if at all!) If you decide to get an agent to get you more lucrative roles just remember that agents take commission from the roles that they book you. If you want to pay for training, information, or materials, that's one thing. But no legitimate agency is going to charge you up front for the joy and privilege of working for them.

- **www.entertainmentcareers.net**
- **www.backstage.com**
- **www.reelextras.net**
- **www.mandy.com**
- **www.indieclub.com**
- **www.talentsoup.com**

Get a Random Job during Various Seasons

These types of jobs are more available during certain times of year. I've known plenty of "sun followers" who would work the tourist season during the summer in Michigan, and then work the ski season during the winter in Colorado. These jobs don't focus on the tourism industry, rather are things you can do in your own hometown, depending on the time of year.

Lifetouch Studios (www.lifetouch.com). Working with Lifetouch, you'll go into various schools to take yearly photos of the staff and kids.

H&R Block (www.hrblock.com). My Aunt Bea worked for H&R Block and so can you! They will provide all the training, and you can make a great income during tax season.

Cruise Line work. If you live in a port city, there are plenty of cruise lines (national and international) that need assistance with checking in guests, baggage handling, and other port-side tasks. Of course if you're feeling adventurous, you could get a job onboard as a chef, housekeeper, concierge, wait-staff, entertainer, photographer, or in any number of roles. Check out **Carnival.com**, **Princess.com**, and other cruise lines for more information.

Local stadium work. Stadiums and arenas employ hundreds of temporary and season employees to work concession stands, clean restrooms, empty trash, and sell merchandise. It can be crazy and hectic (I've worked concessions before) but you'll be able to get into games, concerts, and events for free. Contact your local stadiums to see what the hiring process entails.

Adventure jobs. If you're looking for something a little more adventurous, then you need to check out **www.coolworks.com**. They have job listings for kayak tours, adventure vacations, hiking, rock-climbing and more. These generally revolve around tourist seasons, and may require you to travel outside of your local area.

Umpire and referee jobs. One of my first jobs while in high school was to be a scorekeeper for the local parks and rec department. Some places provide training, and it's a great way to watch games while making some extra cash.

Farmers Markets and Art Shows. During the summer months there are a host of local artists and farmers who need help managing their booths. Look for ads, or visit markets to inquire about work.

Get a Random Job with the Government

The government has many random and temporary jobs just waiting to be filled. Check out your local county and state government websites for job listings and requirements.

U.S. Census (www.census.gov). I worked for the 2000 census and was hired for the 2010 census as well. What most people don't know is that the Bureau of the Census hires workers year round to conduct interviews, although, most of their temporary hiring is for the decennial count. As a census worker, you'll be verifying addresses, following up with people who didn't fill out their forms, and filling out a whole bunch of lovely government paperwork. Generally your assignments last for three to six weeks, with the ability to be called back when more work is available.

Local elections work. Many election positions are paid, not volunteer! I've worked several election cycles through my local government doing various tasks like answering phones, pulling ballots, sending proofing voter pamphlets, voicing the audio ballots, and working the election poll centers. Check with your local county election office to see when they're hiring. Most cities have elections several times a year so you might get some fairly consistent work.

Traffic counter. Traffic counters are needed to determine traffic patterns, gauge the health of the roads and to assist the planning department with expansion or repairs. The job generally consists of setting up counters and rubber hoses (that cars drive over) and may require time on the road in remote areas. Each state is different, so contact your state's department of transportation to get information on how they do traffic counts and the hiring process involved.

Get a Random Job if You Are or Become Disabled

If you have a disability, and the options I have presented so far are not suitable to your situation, there are a few more resources for you to look into the following:

Job Hunting for the So-Called Handicapped. This book by Richard Bolles (the *What Color Is Your Parachute?* guy) goes over the intricacies of the Americans with Disabilities Act and provides advice for those seeking employment, and those wishing to hire.

The National Telecommuting Institute. This organization's mission is to assist those with disabilities in finding work-from-home jobs. Visit their site at **www.nticentral.org**.

Community Options Inc. supports people across the United States with disabilities in their search for housing and employment. Visit their site at **www.Comop.org.**

Abilityjobs.com. From their website: "The goal of ABILITYJobs and JobAccess is to enable people with disabilities to enhance their professional lives by providing a dedicated system for finding employment. By posting job opportunities, employers not only exhibit an open door policy, but also demonstrate their responsiveness to affirmative action by genuinely recruiting qualified persons with disabilities."

Part IV

Becoming the Ultimate Business Professional

Chapter 13 Independent Contractor Responsibilities

The nice thing about working for someone as an employee is that your life, in terms of taxes and responsibilities, is pretty straightforward. You go to work, you punch a clock, you get a paycheck that automatically calculates your taxes, and generally when you file your returns, you get some money back from the government, depending on how much withholding you claim.

Being an independent contractor means that not only are you the employee, who needs to do the day-to-day work of the business, but you are also the business owner, so you're responsible for tax deductions, sales taxes, licensing, marketing, and keeping track of the logistics of things. It's worth it, however, if you're able to establish a good base of revenue to keep you from succumbing to the cubicle lifestyle!

I do not know all of the ins and outs of tax reporting or business licensing, I prefer to hire people to take care of that for me so I don't inadvertently mess things up. In this section, I will give a general overview on the things you need to know as an independent contractor and small business owner. It's ***your responsibility*** to check with your local government to make sure you abide by all of the laws and regulations in your area.

Business Licensing

Many independent contractors ask me if they need a business license to do their work. In my experience it really depends on the type of business you're doing, if you're hiring employees, and how you want to set up your tax structure.

There are two employment classifications that you should become familiar with.

Employee. This is a person who is hired by a company and has their taxes taken out of their paycheck. Most of the work is done on-site at the company, and the employee has set tasks that need to be completed as part of their job description.

Independent contractor. This is a person who creates their own income and primarily uses their own resources to get work done. They alone are responsible for finding clients and all aspects of building and maintaining their business.

Generally, if you're working as an independent contractor and your clients are paying *you*, you don't have to get a business license. You'll receive a 1099 at the end of the year from your clients, and you'll file your income as a Schedule C ("other income") on your tax returns. Your social security number will be tied to this income, so you don't have to worry about doing separate taxes for yourself and your business.

When I wanted to accept checks or process credit cards as my business name, I was required to get a DBA or "doing business as." I did not get a government-issued tax ID (called an EIN, or "employer identification number") I merely filled out a form at the local county offices, paid $15 and received a certificate that stated I was now a DBA. Instead of my clients paying ***me***, as Bethany Mooradian, they were paying my business: Queen of the Random Job. At the end of the year, I got a 1099, still tied to my social security number, and I didn't have to file separate taxes.

When I moved to a different city and state, however, they didn't have a DBA option. I was required to get an EIN from the government, and register with the state as well as the city. I had to file separate taxes for my business and myself as I had separate tax IDs. I was still able to claim a whole bunch of deductions, but this time it was through the business not for me as an independent contractor.

There are many tax professionals that will help guide you along the way as you set up your business structure for your city and state. They can give you advice on local laws and whether you can remain an independent contractor, or if you need to go the full business licensing route.

Check out the SBA and SCORE for small business resources in your area (**www.SBA.gov, www.SCORE.org**).

Non-compete/Nondisclosure Agreements

As an independent contractor, you are going to be bombarded with a plethora of non-compete and non-disclosure agreements (NC/NDAs). Embrace them. Make sure that you create a few of your own for when you work with clients as well.

In essence, these agreements are legal documents that state you're not going run away with your client's information and use it in any way, shape, or form. You'll honor their confidentiality, you won't create competition, and you won't sell their secret formula to the highest bidder.

I use NC/NDAs and contracts with everyone who comes to work with me. I hired my sister at one point, and I required even her to sign a NC/NDA. My whole philosophy behind this is: "I love you. I want to keep loving you. Let's lay it all out on the line so that we each know what is expected of each other and don't end up in small claims court."

You love your clients, don't you? Don't you want them to keep loving you? Embrace NC/NDAs so no one gets annoyed through miscommunication.

Sales Tax

The tax laws are constantly changing and can be quite overwhelming to the new entrepreneur. Even when I took a sales tax seminar, the presenter could do little to answer my specific questions, (she wasn't familiar with Internet tax regulations) so the only advice I really can give to you is, "Check your local government for rules and regulations." Helpful, isn't it?

Keep in mind that each state and city has its own laws. Some states collect sales tax on grocery items that are prepared in store, but not as packaged goods. Some states collect taxes on services, but not on education. For example: yoga classes can be viewed as education, so they're not taxed, whereas fitness classes are. It really depends on where you are to know what you really need to do.

In most states there is a sales tax on products. You, as the business, collect the sales tax from the customers, and then turn it over to the government. You may need to collect sales tax on items that you ship out of state, you may not. You may need to collect sales tax on digital products that are downloaded out of state or you may not. It really depends on your local laws.

Some states have moved from being a "location based sales tax" to a "destination sales tax." This means that you need to collect taxes at the rate of wherever the item is being ***shipped to***, not where it was ***shipped from***. In the coming years, this will get more and more tricky.

Unfortunately, I cannot give much guidance on this subject. Just know that depending on your business, and depending on your city and state, you may need to collect sales tax. And most importantly, you need to check with your local government to see about what regulations are required in your area. Visit **www.sba.gov** and **www.irs.gov/businesses/small** and contact some of your local small business advisors to get started.

Income Taxes and Deductions

Note: I do not now nor have I ever worked as a tax advisor. All I know about taxes is what I've learned from my own experiences. Make sure you consult a reputable and reliable tax advisor to get informed of the current laws.

Here is what I do know: as an independent contractor (IC), you're responsible for keeping track of your income and expenses. If you have clients you may receive a 1099 form at the end of the year that states the income you made, which will go on your Schedule C. Each company is legally required to send a 1099 form to the government if you make more than $600 in a calendar year. If you end up making $590, the company who gave you that income is not legally required to send you the form, but you ARE legally required to report it as income. Chances are that as an IC, you'll be working for more than one company. Make sure to keep accurate records on what you make from whom.

Luckily, the government loves people who are self-employed. Approximately 85% of all businesses in the U.S. are run by the small business owner. Sure we have our huge corporations, but it's the little pizza guy on the street or the farmers at the Saturday market that really make this country hum. In fact, according to the Census Bureau, in 2010 there were approximately 18,500 businesses with 500 employees or more, and 27.9 million "small businesses" (businesses under 500 employees) with a whopping 22 million of *those* businesses being "non-employer" businesses. Meaning, a business with one employee: the Solopreneur.

Small business, or really, Micro-business is alive and well in America today.

Because of that, good old Uncle Sam is happy to give benefits and allowances to the self-employed. When you are working as an employee you get about three tax deductions: Your home, your kids, charity donations, and interest on your college loans—there may be more, depending on your circumstances, but not much.

When you are self-employed you can deduct everything you need for your business, including: your cell phone, your answering service, your computer, Internet access, printer, ink cartridges, mileage, food for business meetings, entertainment for clients, pens, paper, clipboards, other office supplies, parking fees, utilities, and much more.

Of course, you're going to want to consult a tax professional to make sure that you're deducting all that you can, and that you're doing it in a legal way. I gave up doing my taxes long ago because it was just too confusing. It's worth it to pay someone else, and that fee is tax deductible.

You'll need to keep *excellent* records. Get in the habit of getting receipts for everything you do. Save those receipts. If its business related it may be tax deductible.

I have manila envelopes for each category, and also keep track in QuickBooks, which makes it much easier for my tax accountant to deal with everything. The categories I have for my businesses follow:

Accounting: For my fabulous tax lady, who does all the dirty work for me.

Advertising: For newspaper ads, flyers, Web ads, and other promotional goods.

Art materials: For designing my puppets, and other art goods.

Associations: Dues for any professional organizations that I belong to.

Charities: Donations to my favorite charities.

Entertainment: When I have to schmooze clients, potential clients, and others.

Health: My healthcare costs.

Legal: Any kind of legal fees you have to pay. You may need a lawyer for contract help, submitting copyright forms, drawing up leases, or other issues. And yes, prepaid legal counts!

Mileage: Wherever you go to that's business related, TRACK IT. You get around $0.55 a mile! You do need to show a mileage log, so make sure you keep one in the car.

Office supplies: For pens, paper, printer ink, file folders, etc.

Parking and tolls: When I'm on the road on business and have to pay these fees.

Printing and copying: For pamphlets, brochures, flyers, etc.

Post office needs: Stamps, post office box rental, mailers, etc.

Rent: For my office space. (If you work at home, you can only deduct a room if it is *solely* used for business purposes. Talk to your taxman to see how much.) If you have any storage space for business, this can be deducted as well.

Independent contractor fees: When I have to hire others to get work done for me. I don't hire employees. Too expensive with insurance, taxes, and benefits—blech! I hire independent contractors. They are responsible for their own taxes, not me!

Training/education: Any classes I take, books I buy, or materials that help me learn more about my business.

Travel: When I go on vacation, I make sure it's a working vacation and network with people and businesses on my trip. Then, it's partially deductible!

Utilities: For my office space: phone, cell phone, Internet access, electricity, heat, etc.

Website: Design, hosting fees, maintenance fees, etc.

I'm sure there are other deductions out there that I haven't needed yet that may pertain to your business. Talk to a tax professional to make sure that you're getting the most deductions out of your business. Don't give the government any more money than you have to!

If you're concerned that you'll be cited for not having a positive income, keep in mind that you have about seven years to start making a profit on your business. After about 2 years, they'll expect some kind of growth, and they'll want to see that you're profitable at least two out of every five years. If a significant amount of time passes without positive income (meaning, you have more in income then you do in deductions) then government will consider your "business" a hobby. I would hope that within seven years, you'll have substantial income from your business so that you'd be desperate to find more tax deductions.

How to Apply to Jobs

Once you do your research and find legitimate job offers, you need to actually put your best foot forward and try to get the job! Remember that there are hundreds of other people who are applying for the same random jobs, and you need to make sure that you stick out from the crowd. Keep these essential tips in mind.

While on your search, don't look for "work from home," instead search for "telecommute," "virtual office," etc. Most spammers use "work from home" as a lure. Don't fall for it!

Research the company fully before you contact them. Not only to make sure that they're real, but to get an edge as to the culture of the company, and what they might be looking for.

If you're not sure that a company is legitimate, respond with a fake name and e-mail just to see the type of response you get.

Tailor your resume to what they're looking for. Most people who are posting these random jobs don't care too much about official resumes, but it's good to have some sort of listing of your relevant experiences.

DO NOT tell your sob story. I know that times are tough, but no employer (even if it's just for a random gig) wants to know about how dire your conditions are right now. You want to get a job because you're the right person for the job…not because they pity you.

When approaching a company, be brief and to the point. List your relevant experience, show a little of your personality, include your name ***and phone number***. If they get hundreds of responses, and you stick out, the last thing you want is to play the e-mailing game. If they want you, give them the chance to contact you in the quickest way possible.

Don't use an inappropriate e-mail address. It really surprises me that I have to mention this, (you'd think it'd be common sense) but **xxxsex-egirrl@thisisafakesite.com** or **420madness@thisisafakesite.com** do not project a professional image. I wouldn't hire them. Would you?

Be conversational in your tone, follow whatever instructions they gave for submission, and try to do something a little extra to show your skills or that you did research on their company, and know exactly what they're looking for.

Companies don't care about you and how wonderful you are. The hiring process is long and arduous. They have needs that must be met. It's your job to let them know that you understand their needs and to articulate how you're the best one to fill them.

Understand that they may receive hundreds of applications. There is nothing wrong with following up in a day or two just to verify that they received your application. And there's nothing wrong with following up every week or so until you know that you're being considered or not. You can be persistent without being annoying!

Never, ever, EVER give out a credit report to a company unless you have already been through the application process. Many companies now are asking for credit reports to gauge someone's responsibility and ethics. In some states, this practice has become illegal, so just be aware of your local laws. Scam artists are picking up on the credit reporting phenomenon and asking for reports even before you go on an interview. Some are very clear that you don't need to provide an SSN, just the documents with that part blocked out. When this first happened to me, I thought that the company might be legitimate, but then realized what I would be giving up: every single address I ever had, every single credit card I ever had, every loan I ever had—it's a LOT of information. If you have to give up your credit report to work at a company, make sure it's after the job offer is on the table and you've already researched them to know that they're legitimate. You can also talk to their legal department to see what the information will be used for.

If you end up not getting a job, consider promoting your services, (whatever they may be) or starting your own business! In the next chapter we'll be talking about small business ideas, resources and mini-franchises that can help you get started on the path to business ownership.

Chapter 14
Business Brainstorming

It's a common joke that the word "job" is really an acronym that stands for "Just Over Broke."

When you get a job, the company you work for decides your monetary worth. They'll tell you when you go into work, when to leave, and what you have to do to get ahead.

They'll lure you with transparent carrots like insurance, benefits, and the chance of promotions and raises to make you work harder and longer before either outsourcing your job, or laying you off.

If you have to have a job to make ends meet, fine (we've all been there), but don't make it your only source of income. You'll get nowhere.

This section deals with those of you who want to create sustaining income by being your own boss. If you really want a JOB, put this book down and go work on your resume. Sheesh!

Turning Your Idea into Multiple Income Sources

When I first started writing this section of the book, I followed the path of many authors before me and started compiling a list of business ideas. These included things like starting your own gift-basket company, or house-painting business, or any other thing that you've already heard a thousand times. It then dawned on me that those with an entrepreneurial mindset are never at a loss for ideas.

We are "idea fountains" always coming up with brilliant thoughts about our new grand adventure. Creating a list of possible business ideas is just a waste of both of our times because you already know a lot of things that you'd like to do.

However, if this is your first foray into the entrepreneurial world and you need somewhere to start, head on over to your local library for inspiration. Once you've come up with a few ideas that will work for you, check back here for some practical implementing advice. The point of this exercise is to take your passion and look at it from every aspect to create as many sources of income as possible.

Main product or service. You could decide that you want to run a daycare, be a yoga instructor, run your own home repair company, provide resume services, or create a subscription-based website that focuses on pet care. Whatever your main passion is, this is your main source of income.

Complimentary products or services. These are things that are complimentary to your main source of income. For example, if you run a daycare, maybe you sell parenting books, or children's clothing, or have pre-packaged gifts available for birthday parties. (Parents would LOVE you for that!)

Joint ventures. You can partner with a complimentary, non-competing business to expand your client base. For example, I knew of an aromatherapist who joined forces with a Reiki practitioner to put on a free seminar for all of their clients. They each had time to discuss various aspects of their business and doubled their client base.

Consulting. I've been mystery shopping since 1999 and I'm a pretty good authority on every aspect of the industry. Because of my expertise, I have been hired by various businesses to help train their employees on how to provide excellent customer service; and I've also been hired by mystery shopping companies to learn how to create good shoppers and train them properly! You can take your expertise in your industry and consult with others looking to improve non-competing aspects of their business.

Teaching aspects. I know of a divorce attorney who would hold seminars for couples about to get married, as well as for those already in long-term relationships looking to improve. Likewise, I know of plenty of actors who hold classes on how to audition, and workshops on how to perform for film and on stage. There is a plethora of teaching opportunities within your field.

Intellectual property aspects. There is a wealth of opportunity in selling your intellectual property. You can create CDs, DVDs, training programs, how-to's, images, graphics, inventions, and so much more. Everyone has at least one book in them; tell your story, write your song, create that great idea that everyone must have, and share it with the masses!

Swag aspects. Merchandise! You can create mugs and posters and t-shirts and calendars and Frisbees and bags and more with even just your logo and people will buy it. Reusable grocery bags are especially popular now, and it's free advertising!

Licensing aspects. Whatever business you have, there is always the ability to franchise it. There are always going to be people who want to do the same type of business that you have, but don't know where to start. Licensing or franchising your business model (provided you're successful!) is a great way to expand your brand and earn money.

Creating Apps. Website applications, or "apps" are computer programs for the web or mobile technology like Ipads, and smartphones. If you've ever installed a program on your computer or phone to help you quickly check the weather, or monitor your expenses, or even play a game, chances are, you installed it as an app. With apps, you have to learn the technology for implementation, or partner with someone tech-savvy, but once that's done you can usually make around \$1-\$5 per download.

Residual aspects. You should have two goals to any work that you do: 1) LOVE IT and 2) Create some sort of residual aspect to it. This means you do the work once and get paid over and over again.

What else haven't we covered? Sit down by yourself, or even other business owners, and have a brainstorming session about all the great ways you can make money with your brilliant ideas.

Ways to Make Money Online

Whether you decide to pursue a brick-and-mortar business or just pursue income online, there are plenty of ways that you can make money using the Internet. Some of these ideas can be combined with your main source of income while others can stand alone as a separate way to make money.

Affiliate marketing. This was explored in Part II. As an affiliate you will earn commission off of items that you promote to customers. If you ran a fashion website, for example, you could have links to various stores and products for your viewers. If you wanted to promote products without a website, you can buy ad space with Google Adwords, or through various complimentary websites and just have the ad code link through with your affiliate ID.

Affiliatizing your products. If you have e-books, videos, or other products/services, you can set up your own affiliate program and have a massive sales force do the selling for you. Any digital product can be listed on **www.clickbank.com**, you can go to a large warehouse like **www.cj.com** and **www.linkshare.com** (just be prepared to pay hefty fees) or you can set up your own affiliate program at a lost cost and work to find your own affiliates.

Selling ads. If you have a fairly high-traffic website (at least 10,000 unique visitors a day) or a large mailing list, you could make money by offering ads on your site or in your newsletter.

Google Adwords. You can make money through Adwords by having Google place ads on your website. I go back and forth about this because I think it tends to make a site look less professional, but you certainly can make extra income with Adwords!

Subscriptions. If you have a knack for something and like to write, you can sell subscriptions of your newsletter to people. I receive a newsletter of listings for upcoming grants and such for artists. There is both a paid and free version of the service.

Membership site. Think in terms of dating sites, or other membership-only businesses. You provide access to information provided your members pay a monthly fee.

Flipping websites. If you have Web-design skills and a great idea, you can create websites for the sole purpose of selling them. Many Internet millionaires had a great idea, came up with a site, and then flipped it for a tidy profit. If your site is basic though, it will generally flip for $200–$500 per site, depending on the idea and market.

Squatting on names. Squatting has become less popular over the years and is generally frowned upon, but it's something you can do to make money. If you have a great idea for a domain name, go ahead and buy it and wait for someone to contact you to purchase it. Or you can always approach people to see if they'd be interested in buying it. Keep in mind that many large-name corporations like Starbucks and Nordstrom have a plethora of lawyers, so don't try to blackmail them into paying you for their name and a .tv extension!

Joint ventures. If you have a product or service, and someone else has a massive, targeted, mailing list, then you should join forces and work together to make a profit. There are plenty of people who are looking to joint venture with you, provided you conduct your business with integrity and have good products to sell. Don't forget that they're putting their reputation on the line with a list of people that have come to know and trust them over the years!

Web design and Internet marketing. If you have the interest in learning web-design and Internet Marketing, there are a LOT of small business owners who are in desperate need for your help. I taught myself Web design online and through a lot of trial and error. I read about Internet marketing on nearly a daily basis. People recognized that I knew some things and just started hiring me to help them get their websites into this decade. If you have a knack, there is plenty money out there for you to earn!

Chapter 15
Marketing and Promotion Tips

As a small business owner or independent contractor, you are going to have to find clients! And that means you need to learn how to market yourself and your business. It doesn't matter if you're selling on eBay, working as a freelance writer, or just finding companies who will hire you to do random work. You need to be able to sell yourself, your skills, and your products.

What many people don't realize is that more than half of your start-up costs should go into marketing and advertising. A lot of people have the "If I build it, they will come" mentality, and this is why so many businesses fail. In order to be successful, you need to find your niche, know your target market and what they need, and develop a clear marketing plan on how to get it to them.

Businesses fail not necessarily because they have bad products, but because they were unable to deliver their message to the right audience in an effective manner.

For example, if you're selling products online then you need to learn about online marketing. You have to learn where your target market hangs out, the sites that they visit, and the articles that they read. You need to know how to write compelling sales-copy, and create attractive Web pages and flyers. Once you know this information, you can tailor your message to suit their needs in a manner that appeals to them.

If you're selling your services, then you need to find out who the people are that need those services, and get yourself in front of them. You don't necessarily need to be bigger than the other companies who do what you do, just develop a unique niche and be the best within that niche.

Marketing is a deep and complex subject, and more options for getting your message out there are popping up every day (if not every hour!). Take the time to do your research and remember that learning marketing techniques should always be a part of your business strategy.

At the very least start by checking out books at your local library, or going online to research marketing articles for your specific industry. Don't over analyze, though. Get out there and try various techniques, otherwise you'll never get off the ground!

20 Tips to Get You Started

1. First, there is no use in doing any sort of advertising if you don't track it! You need to know how your customers heard about you, so that you can focus on the systems that work. Don't waste your money; keep track of those ads! Get a binder or a folder, and create a separate page for each ad. Make sure that you have a copy of the ad from the source, either the line ad from the newspaper, the postcard that you sent by direct mail, the script from the TV or radio spot, or whatever you chose to do. Date each ad, and ASK YOUR CUSTOMERS how they heard about you. Mark that down in the ad book, and when it's time to renew your ads, (or the end of the month, or whenever you take the time to review this experiment) note which ads were most effective. This will help you put your money in your most effective campaign.
2. If you're going to put up signs around town, check out bookstores, cafes, restaurants, grocery stores, hardware stores, and college campuses for posting areas. When you create your flyer, make sure it has tabs for people to take your information. The worst thing that can happen is that you just have one full page of information, and five minutes after you leave, someone takes that flyer. No one else will see it!
3. Make sure that you post your flyers on Thursday or Friday (that's when most people go out to eat, do grocery shopping, etc.), and check back EVERY WEEK. Yes, it's a pain, but people will move your flyer, cover it up with theirs, or take it down. If you want to get the word out, you need to be diligent.
4. There are a ton of event listings online that you can take advantage of. List your event on **www.craigslist.org, www.eventsetter.com, www.zvents.com,** and check around your local radio, television news, and blogs for event calendars.

5. If promoting online is something that you want to explore further, get involved with **www.facebook.com** and **www.twitter.com.** They are two sites that are great for finding people interested in what you have to say, either locally or nationally. Get involved and get going!
6. Attend networking meetings in your area. Most cities have a small business networking group where you can meet other people who are self-employed. Look through the business section of your newspaper for upcoming events and meetings and check with your chamber of commerce. **www.Meetup.com** is a great resource for finding others with your interests to meet with locally, and **www.LinkedIn.com** has groups that you can join online for networking opportunities.
7. Speaking of which, you should think about joining the Chamber of Commerce in your area. They also have networking events, provide excellent information within your city, and lend credibility to your business.
8. Teach in community education courses. This is a business in and of itself, but really, you can use it to find potential customers. Most centers frown upon selling or promoting your business in any overt way, but what you can do is offer your students to be on your mailing list, and then keep in touch with them. They already know you, and know that you provide good information in the subject of your expertise, so why not keep in touch with them to inform them of other things you're doing?
9. Once you have customers, get their e-mail addresses. I cannot stress how easy and CHEAP e-marketing is. Consider that with traditional marketing, you have to create a flyer, get it printed, and then mail it out to your list. With e-marketing, you can create a fun flyer and send it out over e-mail. It saves time and money. And, these people are the ones who have already done business with you, so they are the best people to promote other events that you have.
10. Current customers are the best source of NEW customers. How many times have you heard someone trying to refer you to their doctor, accountant, hairdresser, or whatever? When customers like you, they'll sing your praises to high heaven. So, come up with ways to keep your customers happy! This could be

something like sending them holiday cards, birthday discounts, customer appreciation discounts, and the like.

11. Have your customers do your marketing for you! Some businesses offer incentives for their customers to give them referrals. You don't necessarily have to give them money, but a discount coupon, free meal, or just a nice note might be enough to expand your reach.
12. Write articles about your field of expertise. After you write, you'll need to submit them to article submission websites (yes there are such places). There are a lot of sites that need content (think of how many articles go through Yahoo during the day) and webmasters who are looking for information in your field will browse to pick up content for their site. The key to writing articles is to keep it clear and concise, and always have your information, with your Web address, at the bottom of each article. You want it as easy as possible for people to reprint your articles, so make sure you don't have any, "contact me for reprint information" disclaimers. You WANT people to share your information as quickly and easily as possible.
13. Consider doing joint ventures. Find a business that has complimentary but non-competing services or products, and brainstorm about how you can work together to expand forces. I've seen physical therapists join with Pilates studios, bankruptcy attorneys join with estate planners, moving companies pair up with retirement homes, and so much more. When you work with others you expand your knowledge base and can double your potential clients!
14. Consider having a free seminar. You can generally rent out a hotel banquet room for a few hours, and put together a seminar that will highlight your expertise and products. Make sure you give good information though; no one likes going to hear a sales pitch for two hours. For example, if you were a mortgage broker, you could have a free seminar regarding refinancing or any other aspect of the mortgage process. At the end of the evening, you can tell people about your services, and how they fulfill all the benefits that you outlined, or at least offer them a chance to be on your mailing list for future seminars, and market to them on the back end.

15. Have a "refer a friend" link on your site and articles. This is HTML or PHP code pasted into your site that allows people to e-mail others about your website. It's instant gratification. When people read your articles, or see your site, visitors may be inclined to inform others about what they learned, but as time passes, they'll forget. When you have this code, people can just enter in their friend's e-mail address, and you get more traffic! You won't receive the e-mail address that your visitors type in, but other people will know about your site and articles.
16. Research has found that you need to contact your mailing list at least every 21 days. After that time, your customers and potential customers forget who you are, and how they got on your list. In the world of traditional marketing, this can get quite expensive. Figure at 10,000 names, even a $0.28 postcard once a month for a year totals $33,600! This is another reason why having customers, (and potential customers) opt in to your e-mail mailing list is essential. You don't have to contact your customers just for your "everything must go!" sale, it could be for a new product, a special seminar, a simple thank you, or just to provide some good information. For example, if you ran a nursery, you could have quarterly updates just with the change of seasons—you could mail out tips dealing with winter frost, bugs that invade the garden, flowers that attract birds for the spring, and all sorts of things. Tie those newsletters in with a promotion, and you have marketing gold!
17. One thing that is essential with any marketing campaign is the sense of urgency. People are more likely to take action when they know that the offer is limited. This is not to say that you need to act like those obnoxious furniture stores that are always having "going out of business" sales. Frankly, that reduces your credibility. If you can come up with a legitimate limited time offer, you'll definitely see a response.
18. Give something away for free as incentive for people to join your list. For my mystery shopping website, I offer a quick start look into the business. Information is the easiest thing to give away for free, but if you have a brick and mortar business, you can always offer a contest to win a free product or service.

19. Going to trade shows, art fairs, and other collaborative venues is a great way to give your business exposure. In all honesty, don't expect to make a lot of money from these types of ventures; it's all about expanding your list. Many attendees of these events just want free samples and love picking up brochures and materials—most of this will get tossed. You do need to have promotional materials, preferably those that aren't perishable. Hershey kisses may draw people to your booth, but people will eat them, toss the wrapper, and forget where they got them from. Make sure you have materials like pens, Post-it® notes, magnets, etc. Make sure that your business name and website are clearly visible. People will take swag. They love it.
20. Continuing with trade shows: remember that people won't just give you their information because you look nice, so it's best to have a raffle or contest to get their contact information to notify them if they won. Most companies forget to follow-up with people on these lists—you'll get more business if you follow up with the losers of the contest, and offer them a consolation prize or $5 off their next visit, or something along those lines. It really costs you nothing, it'll keep you in people's minds, and you may just get a few new customers.

Embrace Follow-Up and Create a System

Repeat after me: The sale is in the follow-up. The sale is in the follow-up. The sale is in the follow-up. Almost soothing isn't it?

The general consensus among marketers is that most sales occur after the seventh contact. That means seven e-mails, seven times someone hears an ad, seven times they receive a postcard, etc. If you're a small business owner and you're only doing one or two follow-ups imagine all the business you're losing. There it goes out the door to your competitor. Poof!!

The ideal follow-up process should be systematic (meaning it's done the same way every time) generate consistent results, and require very little effort on your part. It should run on autopilot and have the following items in place:

Your privacy policy: Tell your customers what you are planning on doing with their contact information. You can check out others in your industry to see what is standard. Keep in mind that at some point you may want to sell your business, so be sure that your policy won't prevent you from transferring your customers to the new owner.

How you will collect information: You should have sign-up forms on your website and a physical sign-up sheet in your brick-and-mortar office. You could also choose to purchase mailing lists, do joint-ventures with complimentary, non-competing businesses, and other methods of acquiring new customers and potential customers.

How can customers unsubscribe: Remember the CAN-SPAM laws. You must have something in place to remove people from your mailing list. Online or off, it's required.

What to send your clients: Once you have a mailing list, what are you going to do about it? People generally don't like to be pitched to. If all you're ever sending them is "buy now" e-mails and postcards, they might just get turned off. Here are just a few ideas: newsletters regarding upcoming events and/or important things in your industry; 10 quick tips; FAQs from other clients; Quizzes; surveys and feedback about your business, and of course your upcoming sales and promotions. At the very least, you should gather your customer's birthdays and send them cards with discounts on products and services during their birthday month.

The Parts of a Cost-Effective Marketing Campaign

E-mail marketing. Always gets your customer's, client's, and prospect's e-mail address. Email campaigns are the cheapest to implement, and you can test various headlines and offers to see what gets the best results quickly.

Phone. Most people are trained to recognize follow-up phone calls as telemarketing and are really turned off by it. You need to approach them as though you're looking for help, gathering information on their recent purchase, or just calling to say thanks. Once you've developed a certain level of trust with the phone call, then you can use it as a marketing tool.

Direct mail. You can send postcards of timely offers, discounts, birthday cards, or just to inform people of what is new in your business. I heard of a car-salesman who would send out greeting cards every month—EVERY MONTH—to all of his clients. The cars were funny and light, and had nothing to do with making sales. But, you can believe that he was extremely successful and received a lot of repeat business, as well as referral business from this plan.

Social Media. I'm one of those rare marketers who doesn't believe that everyone needs to jump on the social media bandwagon. After all, social media will only benefit your company if your target customer is using it! The key is to create a very specific "ideal customer" profile, find out which sites they use, and then move your business to integrate that platform as part of your marketing strategy. Too many times I see businesses that are spending their life on Twitter or YouTube, when they really should focus their efforts on Facebook or other sites. It really just depends on your specific customers and their interests. However, once you find the sites that your customers love and develop a following through them, social media is a nearly free (and very fun) way of connecting with people who are interested in what you have to offer.

Regardless of how you set up your system, remember that your customer likes to make informed decisions. No one enjoys being "sold" on anything. Whatever path you take with your marketing, make sure that it is consistent and full of good information. People are more likely to buy from those they trust, and if you inform them of the benefits of your products and services, (as opposed to just "pitching" a product to them) they'll be more likely to buy, and refer their friends!

Chapter 16
Why Businesses Fail

Time and time again, I have seen people with good intentions fail at creating their own business. Heck, even I've failed at more businesses than I've succeeded at, but I've learned a lot more from my failures than my successes and gladly share those lessons here:

Jumping in Head First without Researching the Business

Frankly, I've seen people spend more time planning their vacation than their own business. You need to come up with a plan on how you're going to market your products and services, how long it'll take for you to break even, your expenses, if people actually need what you're selling, and learning curve that you need to overcome.

Don't even think about joining a direct sales/ MLM/ network marketing company without thoroughly researching the model and industry. Find out if there have been any complaints filed against the parent company, what others think of the business, and take the time to decide if you like the products. Simple as this: Do your homework.

Unrealistic Goals/Expectations

It takes time to build your skills. It takes time to become a leader. It takes time to develop relationships. Every business, EVERY BUSINESS requires some skill, capital, and time to grow.

So many people are looking to make a lot of money with little effort. This just isn't how business works. Put yourself in a continual state of learning, and open up to new books, methods, and ways of doing things. Create your foundation, and build your business on concrete, not sand. People who have invested time and effort over the long haul are the ones who reap continual profit.

Lack of a Duplicable System

If you're going into business, you want to be McDonald's. Well, in terms of their system, anyway. You want a business that is easy to follow, and has been tried over and over again with success. If you're starting your own company, do informational interviews with others in your industry to see how they do things. You don't want to be out there all alone trying to forge your own path. Noble as it may be, it's longer and rougher terrain.

If you're joining a network marketing company, get a hold of their system. Find out exactly what's required, and if you can actually see yourself following their plan. You don't want a sponsor that's sponsored a million people with none of them being successful. You want to be sponsored by someone who knows how to train leaders. If you have your own ideas, that's great too, but make sure that you follow their proven system first. After all, when you start sponsoring people, you're going to want to have a system in place that will allow others to have success.

Lack of Funding

I've seen plenty of business opportunities that claim it takes $0 to start. They're lying. Not necessarily in an intentional manner, but most fail to realize that a business does need some sort of capital to grow. Marketing materials, training, products, or even just time to learn the business are all necessities. There are plenty of investors and peer to peer lending groups to help you with big or small loans regardless of your business size. Don't let a lack of capital stop you from pursuing your dreams, but likewise, don't charge head first into a business without properly determining how much funding you need, and finding the resources to get it.

Not Tracking Your Progress

I cannot stress enough how important it is to track what you do, and the results you bring. You can't change what you don't know is broken, so get out there and track everything you do: Find out how much you're spending on leads, advertising, and customers. Figure out what your average customer spends: from this you can determine how much you can invest in advertising. If you're prospecting, track the number of times you call someone, and how often you follow up before you get a sale.

Fear of the Phone

When I worked at a direct sales company, I hated coming in and working the phones—hated hated *hated* it! I spent endless hours trying to find a way not to pick up the phone. It was almost crippling. When you're running your own business, you need to develop relationships. If you can't meet face to face then the phone is the next best thing. E-mail is becoming too impersonal, and texting for business is a bit intrusive.

The main source of fear is the unknown. When you think of it, the worst thing that can happen is someone hanging up on you, and then the painful process is over. I honestly recommend just practicing with friends or family, as the more you try it, the easier it will become.

Refusal to Adapt

It used to be that all you needed was a business card or brochure to market to your customers. Now, you need a website, email marketing campaigns, Twitter, Facebook, YouTube, and so much more. There are websites devoted to simply giving reviews on your products, services, and business. Beyond being able to reach and connect with customers, many businesses fail to see changing needs, put themselves ahead of the trends, or even just keep up with the competition. In order to be successful in business, you don't just ask, "What does my customer need/want now?" but what will they want in the future, and how can you anticipate their needs and position yourself to meet them?

Chapter 17
The Joy of Residual Income

Do you ever wonder why writers, actors, and musicians are so wealthy? It's not because they're good at what they do, or because they're attractive or even necessarily talented, but due to a marketing campaign combined with a wonderful thing called "residual income."

Residual income is where you do the work once, and get paid for it over and over again. Most of the time we trade our time for an hourly income or salary, and that's all we get. When you set up a business, the goal should be to find a way to make money no matter where you are, or what you're doing. A writer only has to write a book once, and then he gets paid over and over for that work. The actors in a cheesy TV commercial also get paid over and over just for saying, "Ummmmm, that's delicious!" during a 3-hour workday. No matter what you do, make sure you take the proper steps to protect it by registering your works with a patent, trademark, service mark, or other necessary agency.

There are plenty of ways to create residual income if you just open your eyes to it.

Licensing products, images, music, videos, software, etc. Just about everybody has a million-dollar idea that could be sold on TV infomercials. The 'Slap Chop' or 'The Snuggie' come to mind as recent pop-culture icons, but there are a host of other ideas out there. Put your inner-inventor to work and see what you can come up with. If you don't have any ideas, look through approved patents (check your local library or patent office for resources) and contact the creators for rights. Not every inventor is a good marketer, and a joint venture might be just what you both need to make a ton of cash!

Intellectual property. Not only can you make money through the writing of your own materials, but there are a lot of e-book writers who will license their materials to you for a fee. These are called "resale" rights and provide you with freedom to market and sell the materials how you wish. Also, if you have created your own IP materials, you can license your seminars, materials, and even your name. Robert Allen (author and real estate investor) has a host of seminars that use his name to teach his methods to students interested in creating income in real estate, the stock market, the Internet, and through "infopreneuring" (the selling of information). He does not need to be at these seminars. The hosts train their instructors in his methods and materials and pass that on to the students. You can bet, however, that Mr. Allen makes a tidy profit when his name is used!

Real estate. You can create residual income simply by owning property. Over time, the value of real estate goes up much more significantly than if you were to put your money in a savings account. If you find properties and rent them out, you can receive monthly income from your renters. Real estate investing is a complicated arena, and I do recommend that you study up and find someone who has done it so you can learn from their mistakes as well.

Applications. If you have software development skills (or know of someone who does that will work with you) you can create "apps" for the I-phone, Facebook, and a host of other products. People love their apps: be it for weather, games, food tracking, or just silly little things to pass the time. Usually these apps sell for $2 or less or for donations only. Quite a few people have made good money from just playing around with their software skills.

An Anecdote about Intellectual Property

Did you know that "Happy Birthday," arguably the most-recognized song in the English language, is actually copyrighted?

As the story goes, the song began as "Good Morning Dear Children" created by two sisters, Patty and Mildred J. Hill, while teaching at their elementary school in the late 1800s. The lyrics changed to "Happy Birthday to You" and was copyrighted by Preston Ware Orem for the Summy Company. In 1998, apparently the rights to the song were sold to the Time Warner Company, which now enjoys receiving approximately $2 million per year in royalties, splitting with the Hill Foundation.

You can learn more about the song's history at **http://www.snopes.com/music/songs/birthday.asp.**

Why I Love MLM and Direct Sales

So you want to get out of the rat race, you want to have more time to do things that you want to do, but you still need money. You want to have the freedom of being self-employed, but you don't know what kind of business you'd be good at, and the whole McFranchise idea hasn't quite grown on you. Perhaps it's just too expensive, or maybe you just don't like the idea of dealing with 16-year-old kids who are more concerned about their pimples than your fries.

Enter Network Marketing, Stage Left

Some of you have probably already had an experience with MLM, network marketing, or direct sales. Perhaps your uncle was selling Amway, maybe your neighbor was an insurance salesman. Maybe you've been involved with it in some form, and it left a bad taste in your mouth. Regardless, we're going to clear up some of the myths surrounding these types of opportunities.

MLM, direct sales, and network marketing ARE NOT pyramid schemes! To be a pyramid scheme, the company only sells "memberships" (at a hefty price) with no products, no services, no nothing. You are REQUIRED to find other people who will buy into this, earning part of their membership fee as your commission. The more people recruited, the more money you make (in theory).

This is illegal. It is not good. Don't do it.

A lot of people assume they can "get rich quick" with MLM, direct sales, and network marketing. In truth, it's more "get rich slow with lots of effort." You will have products that you purchase wholesale and then mark up to your customers. Examples of this are Avon, Tupperware, Votre Vu, etc.

You'll have to pay a start up cost, and buy your products. You still have to cover marketing and promotion costs. If you find other people who want to sell your products, you earn a slight commission off of what they sell. This is not a scam. It's a brilliant way to leverage time.

Think about when you were a kid, and you had to sell stuff for your school. (I've sold everything from oranges, to wrapping paper, to candy and nuts.) Did you do it alone? No, of course not. You gave a catalogue for your Mom to take to work, your Dad to take to work, and, if you were lucky to have a big family, you enlisted the help of aunts, uncles, grandparents, neighbors, and anyone else who was willing. Sure, one person can sell a certain amount of things, two can sell more, and so on.

The income potential is enormous. If you love your product, and believe in it, learn some marketing basics, and have a great "up-line" (those who train you), your chances of success are HUGE.

Nearly every industry has some company that offers an MLM-type business opportunity, anything from telephone services, health products, kid's toys and books, beauty products, Internet services and so much more. MLM, network marketing, and direct sales have legitimate business plans that really allow you to have the freedom you need, offering products and services that people seek. It's not just selling to your friends and family—with the Internet, there is a world of opportunity out there.

If you're interested in direct sales/MLM, you absolutely need to read Richard Poe. He wrote a series of Wave books (*Wave 3: The New Era in Network Marketing, Wave 4: Network Marketing in the 21st Century,* and more) that outline the history of direct sales and how it has evolved today. It's a great source of information and advice from people in the industry who have been there.

The end of this book has a nearly comprehensive listing of various direct sales and MLM companies. If you find one that interests you, I encourage you to contact a rep in your area for more information.

Chapter 18
Small Business Resources

Inspiration, Guidance, and Support

www.QueenoftheRandomJob.com — Articles, resources, scam alerts and more. Be sure to sign up for the newsletter which gives updated information on companies and scams to watch out for.

www.BuzzyRecommends.com — My recommendations of companies, services, training, books and everything you need to get started in creating income from home.

www.Soloprenerds.com — Launching in 2015, this site is poised to help the solopreneur navigate the world of being self-employed.

www.springwise.com—Tons of entrepreneurial ideas and advice.

www.startupnation.com—Advice, support, business ideas, and local groups.

www.entrepreneur.com—Advice, support, franchise listings and business opportunities. The online voice of *Entrepreneur Magazine*.

Networking

www.BNI.com—Business Networking International has groups in major cities that hold weekly events. Members are required to pay a fee and only one member per industry is allowed in each group.

www.LinkedIn.com—While I consider LinkedIn to be more for business professionals than entrepreneurs, they do have a number of groups and articles geared towards the self-employed.

www.Meetup.com—Although not geared specifically towards business, Meetup has a lot of groups in nearly every interest. Search for your city and business groups and you'll be sure to find something that is of interest to you. Meetup.com itself is free; each individual group may require fees for membership or to attend events.

www.uschamber.com—You can find local chamber of commerce organizations through the U.S. Chamber. The Chamber of Commerce holds events and seminars for its members.

Check out your local area for other groups and trade organizations within your industry.

Business Groups to Help You Out

www.sba.gov—The mission of the Small Business Administration (SBA) is to "maintain and strengthen the nation's economy by aiding, counseling, assisting and protecting the interests of small businesses and by helping families and businesses recover from national disasters."

www.onlinewbc.gov—"OWBO promotes the growth of women-owned businesses through programs that address business training and technical assistance, and provide access to credit and capital, federal contracts, and international trade opportunities....At every stage of developing and expanding a successful business, the Office of Women's Business Ownership is here to counsel, teach, encourage and inspire."

www.score.org—Small business mentoring and training developed through the SBA. They hold workshops and events geared towards small business owners, and provide free mentorships.

www.toastmasters.org—Does getting up in front of a group to give a speech make your knees get weak and your heart race? Do you equate the thought of hundreds of eyes staring at you, and hanging on your every word with a fate worse than death? Get involved with a supportive community that will allow you to break bad speaking habits, and make you more comfortable in front of an audience. I also recommend acting classes through community education to help you gain confidence necessary in business.

Legal Resources

www.uspto.gov—If there is a name, logo, or phrase that you'd like to OWN, consider getting a trademark or copyright. This process is involved and expensive, so be sure that it's something you actually want or need for your business. Do a search through www.uspto.gov, to see if it's already been registered, and if not, go for it!

www.irs.gov—Oh, come on now, you know that if you're going to be self-employed or run your own business, you have to deal with Uncle Sam on a more frequent basis. This link guides you through everything you need to know in terms of government rules. In addition, you get the forms for EIN numbers (if you need a separate tax ID for your business), W-9 forms (if you hire independent contractors), and a sales tax ID form. Check out your state's website for specific regulations.

Funding Sources

www.takecommand.org—Fee-based organization with resources and information that uses fees and advertising as funding for its members. Its "great funding database" has over 5000 names of local, regional and national funding sources for entrepreneurs.

www.fundinguniverse.com—Connects entrepreneurs with active venture capitalists and angel investors. It also helps entrepreneurs create business plans and pitches, preparing them for the investing process.

www.sba.gov—The Small Business Administration division of the Federal government also gives out loans to small businesses that meet their qualifications.

www.gobignetwork.com—From the website: "The Go BIG Network allows professionals to connect with small businesses, entrepreneurs, investors, customers, vendors, employees and advisors. Their website is like a "virtual rolodex" that entrepreneurs can use at any time to connect for help."

Crowdsourcing websites — These sites allow you to post a project and have others chip in to help reach your goal. Check each site individually for regulations and fees.

- **www.GoFundMe.com**
- **www.Indiegogo.com**
- **www.Kickstarter.com**
- **www.Peerbackers.com**

Don't forget about peer-to-peer lending sources like **www.prosper.com** and **www.zopa.com** to find funds to help start or grow your business.

Reputation Management

Reputation management is essential to both individuals and companies. As you start applying for jobs, your potential employers will be searching for you to see if you are who you say you are. And, if you decide to venture into your own business, monitoring your customer feedback and keeping track of your brand's reputation will be imperative. Learn how to see what people say about you, your industry and your company by setting up Google Alerts for your specific keywords. If it's too much to monitor by yourself, you can work with a company who will do it for you. Visit **Reputation.com**, **ReputationChanger.com**, and **Steprep.com** for more information on the services they provide.

Books to Feed Your Mind

Charlie "Tremendous" Jones once said, "Five years from now, you'll be the same person you are today except for the books you read and the people you meet." I highly encourage you to get out there and meet those in business to help you find your way, and read many books to expand your way of thinking.

If you're not financially able to expand your book collection at the moment, then head over to your local library. At some point, however, you're going to want to own these books in every sense of the word. You'll be surprised how, over time, you'll learn different things when re-reading the same words.

Here are just a few books that have influenced and bettered my life, relationships, and business:

The 7 Habits of Highly Effective People—Stephen Covey
The 9 Steps to Financial Freedom—Suze Orman
80/20 Principle – Richard Koch
Art Marketing 101—Constance Smith
Before You Quit Your Job—Robert Kiyosaki
Career Success without a Real Job—Ernie Zelinski
Cashflow Quadrant—Robert Kiyosaki
Celebritize Yourself—Marsha Friedman
Courage to Be Rich—Suze Orman
Do What You Love, The Money Will Follow—Marsha Sinetar
Feel the Fear and Do It Anyway—Susan Jeffers
Financial Peace—Dave Ramsey
Guerilla Marketing—Jay Conrad Levinson
How to Win Friends and Influence People—Dale Carnegie
Millionaire Next Door—Thomas J. Stanley
Multiple Streams of Income—Robert Allen
Multiple Streams of Internet Income—Robert Allen
One-Minute Manager—Kenneth Blanchard
Permission Marketing — Seth Godin
Power of Focus—Jack Canfield, Mark Victor Hansen, Les Hewitt
Refuse to Choose—Barbara Sher
Rich Dad, Poor Dad—Robert Kiyosaki
Secrets of the Millionaire Mind—T. Harv Ecker
The Starfish and the Spider —Ori Brafman and Rod A. Beckstrom
Superaffiliate Handbook—Rosalind Gardner
Think and Grow Rich—Napoleon Hill
Total Money Makeover—Dave Ramsey
War of Art—Steven Pressfield
Wave 3: The New Era in Network Marketing —Richard Poe
Wave 4: Network Marketing in the 21st Century — Richard Poe
Who Moved My Cheese? —Spencer Johnson
Wikinomics —Don Tapscott
Your Marketing Sucks—Mark Stevens

Chapter 19
Direct Sales, Network Marketing and MLM Companies

These businesses are in essence, "mini franchises" since they are start-up friendly in terms of pricing and systems to follow. You can find detailed descriptions of each company along with pictures, and real people who will help you get started on my website: **www.QueenoftheRandomJob.com** under the "Opportunities" tab. There are plenty of established businesses in a variety of fields. And while these companies have been chosen because of their reputation in the Direct Sales industry and many have annual revenues of $100 million or greater, (according to the Direct Marketing Association) please be sure to do your research before you decide to join any company in business.

ACN Inc **www.acninc.com**
Telecommunications

Advocare **www.advocare.com**
Nutritionals, health and wellness

Agel **www.agel.com**
Nutritionals, health and wellness

A Perfect Party by Cody **www.perfectpartybycody.com**
Party packs for entertaining

Alpha Pet Products **www.alphapetproducts.com**
Pet products

AmeriPlan **www.ameriplan.com**
Supplemental healthcare

Amway **www.amway.com**
Nutritional supplements, cosmetics, cleaning products and more

Angela Moore **www.angelamoore.com**
Hand painted jewelry, accessories and gifts.

Annasa Incorporated **www.annasa.net**
Nutritionals, health and wellness

Arbonne International **www.arbonne.com**
Skin care and beauty products

Avon **www.avon.com**
Skin care and beauty products

Azante Jewelry **www.azantejewelry.com**
Handcrafted jewelry made with gifts from the Earth

Bella Handbags **www.bellahandbags.com**
Purses and accessories

Beyond Organic **www.livebeyondorganic.com**
Organic food and beverage delivery

Body Shop at Home **www.bodyshopathome.com**
Bath and body products

Cello in a Box **www.celloinabox.com**
Crafts and gifts

Charmed Moments **www.charmedmoments.com**
Heirloom jewelry

Clever Container **www.clevercontainer.com**
Home organization products

Close to My Heart **www.closetomyheart.com**
Scrapbooking and stamping

Cookie Lee **www.cookielee.com**
Fashion Jewelry

Commission River **www.commissionriver.com**
Telecommunications

Creative Memories **www.creativememories.com**
Scrapbooking

CutCo **www.cutco.com**
Kitchen wares and cutlery

Disciple's Cross **www.disciplescross.com**
Faith-based products

Discovery Toys **www.discoverytoys.com**
Educational toys

Doterra **www.doterra.com**
Health and Wellness

Edible Ecstasy **www.edibleecstasy.com**
Adult and Romance products

Elements Home Spa **www.elementshomespa.com**
Bath and Body products

Entertain with Ease **www.entertainwithease.com**
At-home entertaining products

Fantasy Inc. **www.fantasyinc.net**
Adult and romance products

Fascinations **www.fascinations.net**
Adult and romance products

Five Linx **www.5linx.com**
Telecommunications

Forever Living **www.foreverliving.com**
Nutritionals, health and wellness

For Your Pleasure **www.foryourpleasure.com**
Adult and romance products

Fortune High Tech Marketing **www.fhtm.com**
Technology and communications

Freelife **www.freelife.com**
Nutritionals, health and wellness

Global Domains International **www.website.ws**
Website services

GNLD **www.gnld.com**
Nutritionals, health and wellness

Hanky Panky **www.hankypanky.ca**
Adult and romance products

Healthy Pet Net **www.healthypetnet.com**
Pet Products

Herbalife **www.herbalife.com**
Nutritionals, health and wellness

Inspired Aroma **www.inspiredaroma.com**
French Press, Tea Infusers, Roasters, and Espresso Products

I Remember When **www.irememberwhen.com**
Scrapbooking products

Isagenix **www.isagenix.com**
Nutritionals, health and wellness

Jafra **www.jafra.com**
Skin care and beauty products

Jordan Essentials **www.jordanessentials.com**
Bath and Body Products

Juice Plus **www.juiceplus.com**
Nutritionals, health and wellness

Kyani **www.kyani.com**
Health and Wellness

Latasia **www.latasia.com**
Fashion Jewelry

Legal Shield **www.legalshield.com**
Legal services

Lia Sophia **www.liasophia.com**
Fashion Jewelry

The Longaberger Company **www.longaberger.com**
Handmade baskets, jewelry, home decor

Love Boutique **www.loveboutique.biz**
Adult and romance products

Mannatech **www.mannatech.com**
Nutritionals, health and wellness

Market America **www.marketamerica.com**
Nutritional supplements, cosmetics, cleaning products and more

Mary Kay Cosmetics **www.marykay.com**
Skin care and cosmetics

Melaleuca **www.melaleuca.com**
Nutritionals, health and wellness

Memory Works **www.memory-works.com**
Scrapbooking

MonaVie **www.monavie.com**
Health and Nutritionals

MPB Today **www.mpbtodabusinessopportunity.com**
Home products

Nature Rich **www.naturerich-inc.com**
Nutritionals, health and wellness

Nature's of Scandinavia **www.naturesofscandinavia.com**
Nutritionals, health and wellness

Nature's Sunshine **www.naturessunshine.com**
Nutritionals, health and wellness

Neways **www.neways.com**
Health and wellness, personal care products

Nikken **www.nikken.com**
Nutritionals, health and wellness

Numis Network **www.numisnetwork.com**
Collectible coins

NuSkin **www.nuskin.com**
Skin care and beauty products

Pampered Chef **www.pamperedchef.com**
Kitchen and home products

Park Lane **www.jewelsbyparklane.com**
Fashion Jewelry

Party Lite **www.partylite.com**
Candles

Passion Parties **www.passionparties.com**
Adult and romance products

Primerica **www.primerica.com**
Insurance and financial products

Princess House **www.princesshouse.com**
Kitchen and home products

Pure Romance **www.pureromance.com**
Adult and romance products

Rainbow Vacuum **www.rainbowsystem.com**
Water-trap vacuums

Scent-Sations/Mia Bella's Candles **www.scent-team.com**
Candles and body products

Scentsy **www.scentsy.com**
Candles and Aromatic products

Send Out Cards **www.sendoutcards.com**
Greeting and business cards on demand

Shaklee **www.shaklee.com**
Health, home, and nutritionals

Shure Pets **www.shurepets.com**
Pet products

Silpada **www.silpada.com**
Handcrafted Jewelry

Simply You **www.simplyyou.com**
Fashion Jewelry

Slumber Parties **www.slumberparties.com**
Adult and romance products

Southern Living at Home www.southernlivingathome.com
Kitchen and home products

Stampin' Up www.stampinup.com
Scrapbooking and stamping

Stella and Dot www.stelladot.com
Fashion Jewelry

Surprise Parties www.surpriseparties.com
Adult and romance products

Talk Fusion www.talkfusion.com
Video Communications

Tastefully Simple www.tastefullysimple.com
Specialty food items

Tahitian Noni www.tni.com
Nutritionals, health and wellness

Team National www.bign.com
Home products

Thirty One Gifts www.thirtyonegifts.com
Purses and accessories

Touchstone Crystal www.mytouchstonecrystal.com
Swarovski crystals and jewelry

Tupperware www.tupperware.com
Kitchen and home products

UndercoverWear www.undercoverwear.com
Adult and Romance Products

USANA Health Sciences www.usana.com
Nutritionals, health and wellness

Univera **www.univera.com**
Skin care and beauty products

Usborne Books **www.usbornebooks.com**
Children's educational books

Vitamark **www.vitamark.com**
Nutritionals, health and wellness

Votre Vu **www.votrevu.com**
Beauty and cosmetics

Watkins Quality Products **www.watkinsonline.com**
Earth friendly health and beauty, cleaning and seasoning products

White Lily Candles **www.whitelilycandles.com**
Soy Candles and body products

XANGO **www.xango.com**
Health beverage and nutritionals

Xocai **www.xocai.com**
Healthy Chocolate

Chapter 20
Now What?

Congratulations on making it through this book! Hopefully your head isn't spinning too much from all the information that has been dumped in your lap. You can relax now. You've certainly earned it.

This book is a culmination of over 12 years of trial and error. I have invested thousands of hours and tens of thousands of dollars in books, CDs, training programs, materials, websites, teleseminars, workshops, networking events, business organizations and more. I have started over 10 different businesses (with varying degrees of success), attempted hundreds of different work-from-home and random jobs, and have been scammed more than I care to admit.

By embracing the lessons and information I have put into this book, you have made all of my frustration, debt, discontent, embarrassment, and annoyances worthwhile. I present these materials with the intention that others can learn how to avoid being scammed, and find ways that they can supplement their income.

I hope that I have created some sort of spark and given you ideas to help with your own business so that you can work towards the independence from a traditional work environment.

However, reading isn't enough. It's now time to go forth into the scary work [illegible] ou now have the tools to [illegible]

After all, I got scammed so *you* don't have to!

About the Author

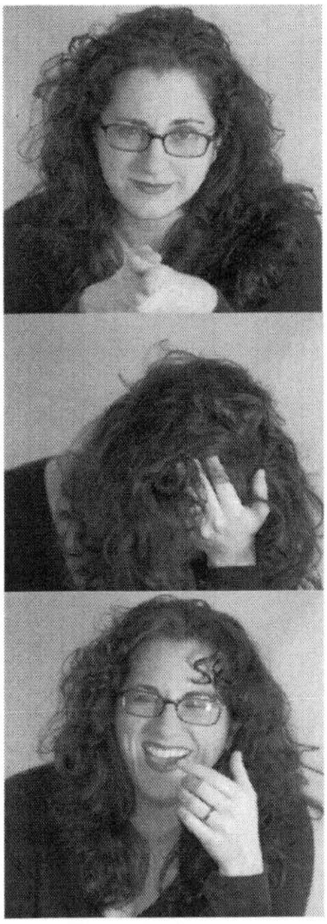

At some point in her life, Bethany has worked as a puppeteer, dog walker, art gallery owner, waitress, child-care provider, book/music seller, actor, sexual health resource clinic advisor, model, baseball score-keeper, customer-service evaluator, merchandiser, mystery shopping company owner, elderly care giver, phone book deliverer, hotel brochure canvasser, pre-school teacher, artist, music and performance venue coordinator, web designer and coder, community education teacher, census taker, election worker, Internet business owner, virtual assistant, standardized test scorer, Pilates studio manager, housekeeper for Bill Gates and Paul Allen, landlord and property manager, vacuum salesman, surveyor, tutor, marketer, project innovator, writer, small business consultant and revenue-generator, and of course, Ronald McDonald's bodyguard.

All of these fabulous (and not so fabulous) experiences have led her to being dubbed, "Queen of the Random Job." After all, she needed ways to supplement her puppetry habit but still find ways to eat!

After over 10 years of trial and error, she has finally found ways to share all of her hard-learned lessons and help others identify scams and find legitimate work. Bethany has created books, training programs, websites and resources to assist others on finding ways to make ends meet and still live their avant-garde passions. Bethany is available for online and in-person workshops and consultations.

Bethany Mooradian
"Queen Buzzy"
www.QueenoftheRandomJob.com

www.QueenBuzzy.com/twitter
www.QueenBuzzy.com/facebook

Also by Bethany Mooradian

The Mystery Shopper Training Program

www.shoppertraining.com

Out of all the random jobs I've done, mystery shopping remains by far the easiest way to earn flexible income. Personally, what I love about mystery shopping is that it can be done anytime and anywhere. (I've shopped in nine different states and two different provinces.) You only take the assignments that appeal to you, and if you need a week, month, or even a year off, it doesn't matter. As long as you do good work, there will always be companies that need your service.

Mystery shopping is an aspect of market research, where you are hired to pretend to be a "real" customer to evaluate products and services you receive. Companies use this information to gauge competition, train new hires, and reward employees. The result is that you get to make money doing a lot of shopping!

Every business gets shopped: apartment buildings, restaurants, banks, retail stores, movie theatres, self-storage facilities, cellphone providers, daycare providers, car rental companies, postal services, grocery stores, golf ranges, hotels, amusement parks, websites, online retailers, healthcare providers, and more!

The Mystery Shopper Training Program gives you all the information you need to get started and keep going as a professional mystery shopper. I've been shopping since 1999, and I've been a shopper, scheduler, and editor. I've taught classes on mystery shopping, consulted with companies, and for two years, ran my own mystery shopping company in the Detroit area. I wrote the book, created the video, and have done every single aspect of this business. If you're interested in mystery shopping, you won't find a more comprehensive program out there!

Also from Moreradiant Publishing

The Repatriate

www.therepatriate.com

In the early months of 1947, eighteen-year-old Tom Mooradian had everything -- Hollywood good looks, high academic ranking in his senior class at Southwestern High School, recognition by the three Detroit daily newspapers as being one of the finest basketball talents in the Public School League and in the state. Before the end of that year, however, he would find himself with hundreds of other Soviet citizens, standing in long unruly lines hoping to purchase a kilo of black, damp, sawdust filled bread. He was fighting the daily fight for survival in the Soviet Union.

But bread was the least of his worries; he was not allowed to travel or utter one word against the state in public or private conversation. Mooradian had lost his freedom. It was not a dream, but a nightmare that he and 150 other American Armenians willingly, but unknowingly, walked into when they signed up for the Armenian Repatriation.

Shortly after their arrival in Erevan, the NKVD, (the Soviet Secret Police) arrested Mooradian as he boarded a plane for Moscow. Beaten at the airport, Mooradian was conveyed to NKVD headquarters, his crime: he had authored and agreed to present a petition, he and three other repatriates had signed, to the US Ambassador, pleading for help to return to the United States.

Mooradian's basketball prowess captured the hearts of the Soviet people and saved his life. Miraculously surviving 13 years behind the Iron Curtain, he had the opportunity to see what no foreign correspondent, no western journalist, no diplomat was permitted to see: the Soviet Union as the Soviets lived.

Filled with political drama, romance, and intrigue, Tom's autobiography, *The Repatriate* reads like a novel, and will have you guessing how Tom managed to return to America alive.

15312372R00105

Made in the USA
San Bernardino, CA
22 September 2014